LEVEL
IX

3RD EDITION

VOCABULARY
FROM
LATINANDGREEK ROOTS
A STUDY OF WORD FAMILIES

By: Elizabeth Osborne

Edited by Paul Moliken

Illustrated by Larry Knox

Prestwick House wishes to extend its gratitude to the many contributors whose assistance, comments, and expertise were essential in completing this book.

Prestwick House

P.O. Box 658 • Clayton, DE 19938
1.800.932.4593 • www.prestwickhouse.com

ISBN: 978-1-58049-202-7

INTRODUCTION

Prestwick House developed *Vocabulary from Latin and Greek Roots* in response to numerous requests for a solid etymology-based vocabulary program. Because the aim of the program is to increase retention of new words as well as to expand students' vocabulary, we chose to organize the Units by meaning rather than alphabetically. A student who associates a root with an idea will be more likely to correctly assess the definition of that root's English derivative.

Each Unit contains at least three Latin and/or Greek roots; one or more English vocabulary words are provided for each root. Unit Five of this book, for example, includes four roots having to do with driving, pushing, and sending forward. When a student reads through the Unit, he or she will see the key letters that signal the presence of each root in an English word. The letters in the third root of Unit Five form the stems PULS, PEL. Beneath the key letters is the root word from which the English is derived: PELLERE, PULSUM. Students will notice that there are sometimes two forms of the root, and sometimes one. The inclusion of two forms indicates a Latin verb from which English has taken two different forms. PELLERE, for instance, gives us the word *propeller*, meaning "a device with rotating blades move a boat or plane forward," while PULSUM gives us words like *pulse*, meaning "an even, steady beat" and *impulse*, meaning "a motivation or incentive." When a root comes from a Latin adjective or noun, only one form will generally be included. Greek roots also appear in only one form.

Beneath the definition of the root, the student will find the word, its pronunciation, part of speech, and English definition. In cases in which an English word has multiple meanings, we have chosen to include only the meaning appropriate to the grade level for which the book is intended. The word *prospect* in this book, then, is a noun meaning "that which is expected," rather than the more familiar verb meaning "to explore looking for minerals, etc."; also in this book, *pedestrian* means "lacking excitement; ordinary and dull," rather than "a traveler on foot." In some instances, students may find it useful to review meanings that do not appear and discuss how they are related to the meaning presented.

If the word has a prefix, or if it is especially difficult to reconcile with its root, the entry will contain an analysis of the parts of the word, followed by a literal definition. *Repulsion* in Unit Five of this book, is explained as *re*, meaning "back," + *pulsum*; the literal meaning is "a pushing back."

Finally, each entry provides a sentence using the word and, when appropriate, introduces pertinent synonyms and/or antonyms. For added visual reinforcement of this understanding, mnemonic cartoons appear in each Unit.

Six different kinds of exercise follow the Unit entries. They include three kinds of practice using words in context, one test of a student's ability to infer information based on a word's meaning, one reading comprehension exercise, and one activity in which a student must deduce the meaning of an unfamiliar word based on knowledge of the word's root. By the end of the exercises in each Unit, students will have had thorough practice using the word in context and will be prepared to make the word part of their working vocabulary.

Note: We have changed the form of some vocabulary words to make the sentences and exercises more interesting, eliminate awkward phrasing, and avoid excessive repetition. For example, a noun (marvel) may be changed to an adjective (*marvelous*) or a verb (*marveled*).

PREFIXES

A (L.) away from
A (G.) not, no
AB (L.) away from
AD (L.) toward
ALTER (L.) another
AMPHI (G.) around, both
ANA (G.) up
ANTE (L.) before
ANTI (G.) against
CIRCUM (L.) around
CO (L.) with, together
CON (L.) with, together *
CONTRA (L.) against
DE (L.) down, down from
DIA (G.) through
DIS (L.) apart, away from
DYS (G.) bad
E (L.) out of
EC (G.) outside
EM (G.) in, within

EN (G.) in, within
EPI (G.) upon
EX (L.) out of, away from *
HYPER (G.) over
IN (L.) in, into, on, against, not *
INTRO (L.) inside
OB (L.) against
OMNI (L.) every, all
PER (L.) through
PERI (G.) around
POST (L.) after
PRE (L.) before
RE (L.) back, again *
RETRO (L.) backwards
SUB (L.) beneath
SUPER, SUR (L.) above
SYM (G.) with, together
SYN (G.) with, together
TRANS (L.) across
TELE (G.) distant

* Note: *con, ex, in,* and *re* sometimes serve as *intensifiers.* In such cases, these prefixes simply mean "very."

PRONUNCIATION GUIDE

a = track
ā = mate
ä = father
â = care

e = pet
ē = be

i = bit
ī = bite

o = job
ō = wrote
ô = port
ōō = proof

u = pun
ū = you
û = purr

ə = about, system, supper, circus

WORD LIST FOR LEVEL IX

UNIT 1
circumspect
elucidate
improvise
invidious
lucid
phosphorescent
photogenic
phototropic
prospect
providential
specter
translucent

UNIT 2
affable
dictum
edict
enunciate
indict
ineffable
infantile
invoke
pronouncement
provocative
renounce
revoke

UNIT 3
abstain
confound
deplete
implement
infuse
inhibit
prohibit
replete
retinue
suffuse
sustain
tenacious

UNIT 4
adept
aptitude
disposition
effigy
figment
formative
impose
inept
misinformation
posit
prefigure
reform

UNIT 5
agenda
delegate
dilate
dispel
exacting
legacy
proactive
propel
relative
repulsion
superlative

UNIT 6
analogous
assonance
audit
auditory
dialogue
disenchanted
dissonance
inaudible
incantation
prologue
recant
resonant

UNIT 7
amiable
amicable
antagonist
antagonize
antebellum
bellicose
belligerence
bibliophile
enamored
philanthropy
philosophical
protagonist

UNIT 8
corporeal
corpulent
divest
expedient
impediment
incorporate
pedagogue
pedant
pedestrian
travesty
vested
vestment

UNIT 9
equilibrium
equitable
homogenized
homonym
iniquity
monogamy
monolithic
monologue
monopolize
unanimous
uniform
unison

UNIT 10
accord
animosity
benefactor
benevolent
benign
cordial
discord
dismal
equanimity
magnanimous
malevolent
malicious

UNIT 11
abjure
aristocracy
bureaucrat
conjure
domineering
indomitable
legislative
legitimize
perjury
predominant
privileged
theocracy

UNIT 12
cadence
casualty
decadent
herbivorous
omnivorous
perceptible
precept
rapacious
rapt
surreptitious
susceptible
voracious

UNIT 13
affluent
alleviate
cede
collapse
concession
elapse
leaven
levity
mellifluous
recede
relapse
superfluous

UNIT 14
amble
ambulatory
consecutive
courier
digress
execution
gradualism
inconsequential
incur
preamble
recurrent
regress

UNIT 15
enjoin
impart
impartial
incision
inclusive
inconclusive
indecisive
injunction
partisan
precise
preclude
rejoinder

UNIT 16
alias
alienate
alteration
altercation
alternate
dissemble
inalienable
metabolism
metamorphosis
metaphorical
semblance
simulate

UNIT 17
antibiotic
biodegradable
immortalize
morbid
moribund
mortify
noxious
pernicious
revival
symbiotic
vivacious
vivid

UNIT 18
anonymous
antonym
cognitive
cognizant
denomination
incognito
nomenclature
nominal
sophisticate
sophistry
sophomoric
synonymous

UNIT 19
affiliate
expatriate
filial
genealogy
maternal
matriculate
matron
paternal
patricide
patronize
progenitor
progeny

UNIT 20
diminish
magnate
magnitude
maxim
megalomaniac
megalopolis
microcosm
microscopic
minuscule
minute

UNIT ONE

PHOT, PHOS
Greek PHOS, PHOTOS, "light"

PHOTOTROPIC (fō tə trō´ pik) *adj.* tending to grow or move toward light
G. *photos + tropein*, "to turn" = *to turn toward the light*
Because they are *phototropic*, daisies always grow toward the sun.

PHOSPHORESCENT (fos fə res´ ənt) *adj.* giving off light without heat
G. *phos + phorein*, "to bear" = *light-bearing*
Harvey stuck *phosphorescent* stars on his ceiling so that it would resemble the nighttime sky.

PHOTOGENIC (fō tə jen´ ik) *adj.* attractive in pictures or photographs
G. *photos + genic*, "suitable for" = *suitable for photographs*
Lucy was so *photogenic* that total strangers often asked to take her picture.

LUC
Latin LUX, LUCIS, "light"

LUCID (lōō´ sid) *adj.* easy to understand; clear
Sophie's explanation of quantum physics was so *lucid* that I understood everything.
syn: comprehensible   *ant: confusing*

ELUCIDATE (ē lōō´ si dāt) *v.* to make clear by explaining
L. *e*, "from" + *lucis* = *to bring light from*
The attorney asked the witness to further *elucidate* the information he had.
syn: clarify   *ant: confuse*

TRANSLUCENT (trâns lōō´ sənt) *adj.* allowing light to pass through
L. *trans*, "through" + *lucis* = *light passing through*
Through a *translucent* blue cloth draped over the window, we could see the sun.
syn: semi-transparent

At night in tropical seas, various small organisms seem to glow if they break the surface of the water. This is known as phosphorescence. In the deep part of the ocean, where there is no visible light, however, many creatures, fish, invertebrates, and crabs emit a glow from different parts of their bodies to attract food or for mating. This process is known as "bioluminescence." Since both processes involve giving off light, what might be the difference?

The official motto of Yale University is "Lux et Veritas"—"Light and Truth."

SPEC, SPECT
Latin SPECERE, SPECTUM, "to look at"

CIRCUMSPECT (sûr´kəm spekt) *adj.* careful; mindful of rules and
consequences
L. *circum*, "around" + *spectum* = *looking around*
The marchers in the protest rally tried to be *circumspect* and not break any laws.
syn: prudent *ant: reckless*

PROSPECT (pros´pekt) *n.* that which is expected
L. *pro*, "forward" + *spectum* = *looked forward to*
The *prospect* of a trip to the dentist with my bratty kid brother was hardly
thrilling.

SPECTER (spek´tər) *n.* a ghost or phantom
Hattie seemed to see a *specter* in every corner
of the dark house.

HECTOR the SPECTER was host of the ghost party.

VID, VIS
Latin VIDERE, VISUM, "to see, to look"

INVIDIOUS (in vid´ē əs) *adj.* hateful or spiteful
L. *in*, "against" + *videre* = *to look against*
One candidate made an *invidious* speech against his opponent.
syn: defamatory *ant: pleasant*

PROVIDENTIAL (prâ və den´shəl) *adj.* happening by good fortune
L. *pro*, "forward" + *videre* = *to look forward*
Through a *providential* series of events, Nigel found himself manager of
the company.
syn: fortunate *ant: unlucky*

IMPROVISE (im´prə vīz) *v.* to create without any forethought or preparation
L. *in*, "not" + *pro*, "forward" + *visum* = *not seen in advance*
When Carl lost the cards with his speech on them, he was forced to *improvise*.
ant: plan

⫼ The word specter, *in
addition to describing
the kind of ghost that
haunts a place, can
describe anything that
haunts or preoccupies
someone. For example,
the specter of war
might haunt an uneasy
world.*

⫼ Providence *is literally
the ability to see in
advance, so the word is
sometimes used as a
synonym for "God."*
Prudence *is a related
word that means
"carefulness."*

EXERCISES - UNIT ONE

Exercise I. Complete the sentence in a way that shows you understand the meaning of the italicized vocabulary word.

1. When Roger thought he saw a *specter* lurking in the corner, he reacted by…

2. I found Charlie a rather *invidious* character because he was always…

3. The actor had to *improvise* his lines because he…

4. I like to say jokingly that my cat is *phototropic* because she always…

5. Nina tried to *elucidate* the meaning of the poem by…

6. Buck savored the *prospect* of the nature walk because…

7. Because he was not considered very *photogenic*, Sven…

8. The headdress was woven of a beautiful *translucent* silk that…

9. Unless something extraordinarily *providential* happens before the swim meet, we…

10. Tom thinks the reason Gerald's explanations are so *lucid* is…

11. Carl was usually *circumspect* when choosing stocks and bonds because…

12. One of the *phosphorescent* gemstones can be identified by…

Exercise II. Fill in the blank with the best word from the choices below. One word will not be used.

providential   circumspect   photogenic   translucent   improvise

1. The delicate, _____ ribbons in the girl's hair seemed to glow.

2. When my first strategy didn't work, I had to _____ a new one.

3. Even the most _____ people don't look attractive in overdeveloped pictures.

4. The one _____ occurrence in Ralph's life was his discovery of the ancient tomb in his back yard.

Fill in the blank with the best word from the choices below. One word will not be used.

     providential   invidious   phototropic   specter   phosphorescent

5.   Scientists were amazed to discover that the plant was not _____ at all and could grow in total darkness.

6.   Dawn can be quite _____ at times; she has started several nasty rumors.

7.   The _____ wandered the halls of the aged mansion in search of a resident to frighten.

8.   The _____ fish emitted a faint glow even at the bottom of the dark sea.

Fill in the blank with the best word from the choices below. One word will not be used.

     lucid   prospect   invidious   elucidate   circumspect

9.   If you are more _____ about your finances, you won't be out of money at the end of the month.

10.   Nick can discuss and analyze history in a clear and _____ manner.

11.   While trying to _____ the book's theme, I made some interesting discoveries.

12.   The _____ of spending the winter on a tropical island was thrilling to Rebecca.

Exercise III. Choose the set of words that best completes the sentence.

1.   After George _____ his plan, the _____ of climbing the mountain became more understandable to me.
    A. elucidated; specter
    B. elucidated; prospect
    C. improvised; prospect
    D. improvised; specter

2.   Daria was upset that she could not provide a(n) _____ explanation of her discussion with the _____ in her nightmare.
    A. providential; prospect
    B. phototropic; specter
    C. lucid; specter
    D. invidious; prospect

3.   The _____ discovery of a new _____ organism helped researchers, who were doing work on light and biology, make a long-desired breakthrough.
    A. photogenic; circumspect
    B. invidious; photogenic
    C. providential; phototropic
    D. translucent; lucid

4.   Although the actor thought he did an excellent job _____ his lines, he received several _____ reviews the next day.
      A.   elucidating; lucid
      B.   improvising; providential
      C.   elucidating; translucent
      D.   improvising; invidious

5.   Even my modest, _____ grandmother became as excited as a child when she saw the _____ white silk with which we would make the dress.
      A.   photogenic; providential
      B.   lucid; phosphorescent
      C.   circumspect; translucent
      D.   invidious; phototropic

Exercise IV. Complete the sentence by inferring information about the italicized word from its context.

1.   If your neighbor becomes *invidious*, you may conclude that…

2.   When a substitute teacher *improvises* a schedule, we can assume…

3.   When buying a new car, it's best to be *circumspect* because…

Exercise V. Fill in each blank with the word from the Unit that best completes the sentence, using the root we supply as a clue. Then, answer the questions that follow the paragraphs.

For nearly two centuries, a man's appearance had no effect on his candidacy for president of the United States. George Washington, the father of our country, had wooden teeth and rarely smiled. Because of a severe visual disability, James Buchanan tended to lean his head to the side. Abraham Lincoln, although known for his height, did not have the sort of _____ (PHOT) face that would attract interest on television. William Howard Taft was a Supreme Court justice, as well as president, but he also weighed over 325 pounds. Franklin Delano Roosevelt could not walk, but his confinement to a wheelchair remained unknown to the public because he communicated with the nation primarily through radio addresses.

All of this changed with the 1960 presidential election, a tight contest between Vice President Richard Nixon and Senator John F. Kennedy of Massachusetts. The tradition of debate between candidates is a rich one in American history, but never before had one of these debates appeared on television. According to reports of the time, Senator Kennedy appeared much more at ease than his rival did. Kennedy used cosmetics to emphasize his suntan, and his confidence and bright smile clearly impressed the television audience. His ability to _____ (VIS) in the middle of this heated debate made him seem collected and relaxed. Vice President Nixon, on the other hand, did not fare well with his makeup. His pale complexion was not suited to television lights, his need for a shave showed through the makeup, and, as the debate went on, he began to sweat. His forced smile and nervous movements also made him appear defensive and confused.

After the debate, two separate polls were taken, one of radio audiences and the other of television viewers. Both asked the same question: Which candidate do you think won the debate? The results were striking. The radio audience thought that Vice President Nixon had won the debate, while the television viewers thought that Senator Kennedy had won. This difference _____ (LUC) an important point about human nature: What we see, more than any other sense, greatly influences our opinions of other people. Clearly, a visual impression of a leader also affects the choice we make at the polls.

1. 1. Which of the following is a synonym of confinement as it is used in the first paragraph?
    A. preference
    B. restriction
    C. insanity
    D. disability

2. Which of the following best summarizes the main idea of this essay?
    A. Tall presidents tend to seem more presidential than short ones do.
    B. Physical appearance does not accurately indicate presidential performance.
    C. The visual sense seems to dominate the others in creating ideas about a public figure.
    D. The television age has made people more superficial in their judgments.

3. Why did the television audience think that Kennedy had won the debate?
    A. Kennedy had a more confident voice than Nixon did on the radio.
    B. Nixon seemed to dislike speaking on the radio more than on television.
    C. Nixon appeared less confident on television than Kennedy did.
    D. Both Kennedy and Nixon showed excellent debating skills.

Exercise VI. Drawing on your knowledge of roots and words in context, read the following selection and define the italicized words. If you cannot figure out the meaning of the words on your own, look them up in a dictionary.

When she sat on the photographer's stool, the entire class was silenced. Lucinda was the most photogenic girl in her school; the camera seemed to adore her. In every portrait, her *visage* was as bright and clear as that of an angel. Everyone who saw the pictures said that her face glowed with enthusiasm and *speculated* as to why this might be the case.

UNIT TWO

NUNC, NOUNC
Latin NUNTIARE, NUNTIATUM, "to announce"

ENUNCIATE   (ē nun´ sē āt)   *v.*   to pronounce or speak clearly
L. *e*, "out of" + *nuntiatum* = *to announce out of*
The spelling bee contestant was asked to *enunciate* so that the judges could understand what she was saying.
ant: mumble

RENOUNCE   (ri nowns´)   *v.*   to reject by declaration
L. *re*, "back" + *nuntiatum* = *to go back on an announcement*
In order to become a member of the fraternity, Jeff had to *renounce* his membership in other organizations.
syn: disavow   *ant: reaffirm*

PRONOUNCEMENT   (prə nowns´ mənt)   *n.*   a declaration of opinion; a judgment
L. *pro*, "forth" + *nuntiatum* = *to announce forth*
Fred's *pronouncement* that the party was a disaster drew agreement from the whole group.
syn: declaration

VOC, VOK
Latin VOCARE, VOCATUS, "to call"

INVOKE   (in vōk´)   *v.*   to call on for support
L. *in*, "on" + *vocare* = *to call on*
Amy *invoked* the First Amendment when Bill tried to silence her.
syn: appeal

PROVOCATIVE   (prə vok´ ə tiv)   *adj.*   causing disturbance or excitement
L. *pro*, "forth" + *vocare* = *to call forth (emotions)*
The film's *provocative* ending had people talking for months.

REVOKE   (ri vōk´)   *v.*   to make invalid; to deactivate
L. *re*, "back" + *vocare* = *to call back*
If you don't pay your traffic tickets, the state may *revoke* your driver's license.
syn: recall, cancel   *ant: activate*

The angry cigarette shouted, "REVOKE the NO SMOKING law!"

▥ *Some Christians believe that the angel Gabriel visited Mary to tell her she would be the mother of Christ. This event is known as the Annunciation (ad, "toward," + nuntiatum).*

▥ *Classical literature often started with an invocation to a Muse (a goddess of poetry or some other art).*

FA
Latin FOR, FARI, "to speak"

INEFFABLE (in ef´ ə bəl) *adj.* unutterable; indescribable
L. *in*, "not" + *ex*, "out of" + *fari* = *not able to be spoken*
Many religious writers speak of the *ineffable* wisdom of the divine being.

INFANTILE (in´ fən tīl) *adj.* childish; immature
L. *in*, "not" + *fari* = *not able to speak*
Although Rachel finds practical jokes funny, Didi finds them *infantile*.
syn: juvenile   *ant: mature*

AFFABLE (af´ ə bəl) *adj.* easy to converse with; friendly
L. *ad*, "toward" + *fari* = *to speak toward*
The principal was an *affable* man who got along well with all the children.
syn: courteous   *ant: surly*

DIC, DICT
Latin DICERE, DICTUM, "to say, to tell"

EDICT (ē´ dikt) *n.* an official order
L. *e*, "out of" + *dictum* = *to speak out (officially)*
The palace issued an *edict* forbidding the rebel prince from entering the country.
syn: decree

INDICT (in dīt´) *v.* to charge with a crime; to accuse
L. *in*, "against" + *dictum* = *to speak against*
The jury *indicted* Richard on seven counts of burglary.
syn: charge   *ant: excuse*

DICTUM (dik´ təm) *n.* a formal or authoritative statement
L. *dictum, having been said*
When asked to defend his argument, Luther cited a *dictum* of his favorite poet.

▥ Did you know that infant literally means "one who cannot speak"? Someone who is infantile, *on the other hand, just acts like a baby.*

▥ Remember that indict is pronounced "in DITE," not "in DICT."

EXERCISES – UNIT TWO

Exercise I. Complete the sentence in a way that shows you understand the meaning of the italicized vocabulary word.

1.   Before you *invoke* a particular law, be sure that…

2.   When the people heard about the cruel king's *edict*, they…

3.   When one debater made a *provocative* comment, his opponent…

4.   Because Henry *renounced* his initial vow to boycott reading the book,…

5.   I could not explain why the wisdom of the holy man was *ineffable*, but,…

6.   If the student giving the report does not *enunciate*, the other students…

7.   The club members voted to *revoke* Zeke's membership because…

8.   I thought Angelo's behavior was *infantile*, especially when…

9.   If Derek believes in the old *dictum* about "practicing what you preach," he will…

10. The newspaper writer *indicted* government officials for…

11. The senators responded to the president's *pronouncement* by…

12. I would characterize Jane as *affable* because…

Exercise II. Fill in the blank with the best word from the choices below. One word will not be used.

revoke	ineffable	invincible	renounce	dictum

1.   The _____ beauty and peace of the ceremony left us speechless.

2.   I always keep in mind a(n) _____ that my mother was fond of repeating.

3.   If Tony's license is _____, he will have to ride with me.

4.   The general of the rebel army _____ his previous allegiance to the government.

Fill in the blank with the best word from the choices below. One word will not be used.

provocative   edict   affable   pronouncement   invoke

5.   Juan, a(n) _____ little boy, loved to sit and talk with his grandmother for hours.

6.   In ancient Rome, wives would _____ the help of the goddess Juno.

7.   There was a formal _____ issued which prohibited people from leaving the country.

8.   Despite Larry's negative _____ on the movie, I decided to go.

Fill in the blank with the best word from the choices below. One word will not be used.

revoke   indict   infantile   provocative   enunciate

9.   Environmentalists _____ the automobile industry for many of the world's pollution problems.

10.   The play was so _____ and anti-intellectual that my roommate staged a protest over it.

11.   Cody needs to _____ his words so he can be understood.

12.   After some rather _____ stomping around, Myra calmed down and became an adult again.

Exercise III. Choose the set of words that best completes the sentence.

1.   One _____ issued by the Church forbade _____ behavior during services.
     A.   pronouncement; affable
     B.   dictum; infantile
     C.   edict; provocative
     D.   edict; affable

2.   My once-_____ and easygoing neighbor now _____ every curse she could think of against me.
     A.   affable; invoked
     B.   provocative; indicted
     C.   affable; renounced
     D.   infantile; enunciated

3.   The religious leader hoped the _____ he cited would convince people to _____ their bad habits.
     A.   edict; enunciate
     B.   pronouncement; invoke
     C.   indictment; revoke
     D.   dictum; renounce

4.   None of my father's _____ on my behavior could prevent my _____ tantrums when I didn't get what I wanted.
     A.   dictums; affable
     B.   dictums; ineffable
     C.   pronouncements; infantile
     D.   edicts; provocative

5.   The Grand Jury felt it necessary to _____ the reporter for refusing to _____ his false statements.
     A.   enunciate; revoke
     B.   invoke; renounce
     C.   revoke; indict
     D.   indict; renounce

Exercise IV. Complete the sentence by inferring information about the italicized word from its context.

1.   If Gerald *renounces* his friendship with Kate, he probably feels that she…

2.   If your employer seems especially *affable* on a certain day, you might think that…

3.   When a child learns to *enunciate* properly, his parents will probably…

Exercise V. Fill in the blank with the word from the Unit that best completes the sentence, using the root we supply as a clue. Then, answer the questions that follow the paragraphs.

When television was first introduced as a medium for communication, there were many strict guidelines as to the content and nature of programming. The rule against kisses of a certain length of time, or of a certain intensity, is only one example. For years, married couples were portrayed in the bedroom sleeping in separate twin beds. Not until *The Munsters* did a married couple appear in the same bed. During this period, writers and producers were forced to edit themselves very carefully.

The television industry also placed firm limits on its writers regarding gender roles. For instance, not only did June Cleaver, the fictional mother on the show *Leave It to Beaver*, stay at home rather than have a job—she vacuumed her house while wearing pearls! *I Dream of Jeannie* revolved around an astronaut and his servant, a slender, blonde, attractive genie named, of course, Jeannie. Although Jeannie wore outfits considered _____ (VOC) in her day, and although she occasionally did things against her master's wishes, she, ultimately, submitted to his authority.

All of this changed in the late 1960s and 1970s. It seemed that most of the creative show ideas had been used, and network ratings were dropping. Network executives were on the lookout for fresh ideas, and a man named Chuck Barris stepped up to provide them. In a show called The Dating Game, he introduced the idea of a single woman question-ing three single men behind a screen and then selecting one as a date. This innovative move to "reality" television, upon which real people and real events were portrayed, was appealing to the networks because the shows had low writing costs. Plots came from real people on the screen, not from the imaginations of producers and writers. Ratings soared for this new type of show, and the Barris format was copied time and time again.

Variation after variation came from the mind of Chuck Barris. *The Newlywed Game* asked couples questions to see how well they knew each other. Reality television showed people at their most _____ (FA) on *The Gong Show*. Billed as a low-level talent show, this program—actually hosted by Barris himself—brought people onto national television to sing, dance, or perform in some other way. When a panel of judges decided the contestant was too bad to continue, they would ring a gong to end the performance.

Reality programs signaled a change in the way that television engaged the minds of its viewers, rather than providing stories and roles that suggested ways for viewers to act and think. Viewers, instead of seeking to be like the people they saw on screen, laughed at these people's shortcomings. As television continues to evolve, one wonders if the nature and purpose of viewing itself will continue to change.

1.   How did television change in the late 1960s and 1970s?
     A.   Writers adopted stricter rules regarding gender limits.
     B.   Shows began to focus on characters instead of real people.
     C.   Television provided new examples for viewers to follow.
     D.   Real people replaced written scripts as a source of action.

2.   Which of the following is NOT true about Chuck Barris?
     A.   He approved of the strict gender roles on television.
     B.   He regularly hosted *The Gong Show*.
     C.   He wanted to change methods of television entertainment.
     D.   He created *The Dating Game*.

3.   What can be inferred from the passage?
     A.   Network executives didn't want to change the way television entertained viewers.
     B.   Network executives wanted to increase the number of children watching their programs.
     C.   Chuck Barris changed the way television interacted with its viewers.
     D.   Acts on *The Gong Show* were usually excellent.

4.   Why were there low writing costs for the new reality shows?
     A.   The shows depended on real people rather than on written scripts.
     B.   The shows were a new form of entertainment that people enjoyed.
     C.   Viewers could interact with the people onscreen in a new way.
     D.   Network ratings were dropping, and executives liked the new idea.

Exercise VI. Drawing on your knowledge of roots and words in context, read the following selection and define the italicized words. If you cannot figure out the meaning of the words on your own, look them up in a dictionary. Note that *ferous* (from *ferre*, "to carry,") means "carrying," and that *ad* means "towards."

A *vociferous* crowd of supporters of a ban on personal handguns marched outside the National Rifle Association's headquarters in Washington, D.C., last Thursday. The noisy protesters claimed that the NRA promoted "free gun use" among Americans. Across the street, a smaller group of personal handgun *advocates* gathered to stage their own demonstration. Fortunately, both sides protested peacefully while also making their views known.

UNIT THREE

HIB, HAB
Latin HABERE, HABITUM, "to have; to hold"

PROHIBIT   (prō hib´ it)   v.   to stop someone from doing something; to prevent
L. *pro*, "in front of" + *habitum* = *to hold in front of*
If the law did not *prohibit* speeding, there would be far more traffic accidents.
                              ant: allow

INHIBIT   (in hib´ it)   v.   to get in the way of; to hinder
L. *in*, "in" + *habitum* = *to hold in*
Jenny decided she wouldn't let nervousness *inhibit* her success in the swim meet.
syn: prevent   *ant: aid*

FUS, FOUND
Latin FUNDERE, FUSUM, "to pour out"

SUFFUSE   (sə fūz´)   v.   to fill up from within; to spread throughout
L. *sub*, "beneath" + *fusum* = *to pour from beneath*
The light of inner peace seemed to *suffuse* the monk's face as he spoke to us.

CONFOUND   (kən fownd´)   v.   to confuse and frustrate
L. *con*, "together" + *fundere* = *to pour together*
Although the twins sometimes *confound* me with their tricks and secret language, we usually get along pretty well.

INFUSE   (in fūz´)   v.   to inject; to fill something or someone with
L. *in*, "into" + *fusum* = *to pour into*
After many losses, the basketball team needed someone to *infuse* it with pride and determination.
                              ant: empty, remove

III Prohibition *is the name given to the period during which alcohol was banned in the United States. The 18th Amendment of the Constitution prohibited commercial trade in alcohol; the 21st Amendment repealed the 18th.*

TEN, TAIN, TIN
Latin TENERE, TENTUM, "to hold"

SUSTAIN   (sə stān)   *v.*   to support for an extended period of time
L. *sub*, "beneath" + *tenere = to hold (from) beneath*
I am amazed that Jeff can *sustain* his family on the tiny amount of money
he makes.

ABSTAIN   (ab stān)   *v.*   to not do something; to refrain
L. *ab*, "away from" + *tenere = to hold away from*
When I *abstained* from watching television, I found I had much more free time.
                        ant: indulge

TENACIOUS   (tən ā´ shəs)   *adj.*   stubbornly
        persistent; determined
L. *tenax*, "holding fast, stubborn"
Thanks to a *tenacious* group of citizens, the
dangerous building was finally torn down.
syn: steadfast

RETINUE   (ret´ in ū)   *n.*   a group that attends
        an important person
L. *re*, "back" + *tenere = that which is retained*
Queen Elizabeth I always had a large *retinue* of
ladies-in-waiting around her.
syn: entourage

The octopus' *TENACIOUS TENTACLES*
held fast to the object of his love.

PLE
Latin PLERE, PLETUM, "to fill"

REPLETE   (ri plēt´)   *adj.*   filled up with
L. *re*, "again" + *pletum = to fill up again*
The ship was *replete* with supplies for the month-long journey.
                        ant: emptied

IMPLEMENT   (im´ plə mənt)   *v.*   to put into action; to execute
L. *in*, intensifier, + *pletum = to fill*
It took the company several days to *implement* the new billing system.

DEPLETE   (dē plēt´)   *v.*   to use up; to waste
L. *de*, "down" + *pletum = to go down from full*
The desert travelers were careful not to *deplete* their precious supply of water.

 The word retain, *from re
+ tenere, means "to hold
back" in the sense of "to
keep." A retinue is a
group of people kept by a
figure of importance or
authority.*

 Be careful not to confuse
replete *with* complete.
Replete *is used only as a
synonym for "full" or
"abundantly supplied."*

EXERCISES - UNIT THREE

Exercise I. Complete the sentence in a way that shows you understand the meaning of the italicized vocabulary word.

1. Since laws *prohibit* the use of cellular phones on airplanes, Merle decided…

2. The sunlight completely *suffused* the room when…

3. If even one person who has pledged to vote for the mayor decides to *abstain*, then…

4. The party table was *replete* with food, so I suspected that…

5. This scientific theory *confounds* George because…

6. Tony was able to *infuse* us with hope by…

7. Brandon was so *tenacious* in fighting the weeds that…

8. If we choose to *implement* a plan that makes sense,…

9. The king always traveled with a large *retinue* because…

10. Because the sailors *depleted* their supply of water, they…

11. If it is heavily farmed, the land will probably be unable to *sustain*…

12. Rita was worried that her sore muscles would *inhibit* her ability to…

Exercise II. Fill in the blank with the best word from the choices below. One word will not be used.

abstain   suffuse   prohibit   retinue   confound

1. After a long run, Sarah was _____ with a happy glow.

2. Julia's strict adherence to the rules of her religion does not _____ her from having fun.

3. Because I was trying to lose weight, I _____ from eating at fast food restaurants.

4. Although these math problems sometimes _____ Rick, most of the time, he finds them enjoyable.

Fill in the blank with the best word from the choices below. One word will not be used.

| retinue | sustain | tenacious | replete | confound |

5.   Both wrestlers were talented, but the more _____ one held out longer.

6.   The pioneer family's wagon was _____ with supplies they hoped would help them on their journey.

7.   I found it hard to believe how long the singer was able to _____ the note.

8.   The wealthy corporate executive never traveled without his _____ of secretaries, assistants, and accountants.

Fill in the blank with the best word from the choices below. One word will not be used.

| implement | infuse | abstain | deplete | inhibit |

9.   If we _____ all of our natural resources, we will have a hard time surviving.

10.   When the company decides to _____ the new schedule, my hours will probably change.

11.   I am afraid that my lifelong fear of heights will severely _____ my enjoyment of the flight to Europe.

12.   The glorious sunrise seemed to _____ Lonnie with hope and purpose.

Exercise III. Choose the set of words that best completes the sentence.

1.   In order to _____ good working relationships between employees, companies often _____ office romances.
     A.   inhibit; infuse
     B.   infuse; prohibit
     C.   sustain; prohibit
     D.   abstain; implement

2.   The large _____ that followed the rock star could _____ him with a sense of personal strength and importance.
     A.   retinue; deplete
     B.   retinue; suffuse
     C.   retinue; infuse
     D.   retinue; confound

3. Good animal trainers know that they can _____ behaviors that will not _____ an animal's personality.
    A. sustain; deplete
    B. sustain; inhibit
    C. suffuse; deplete
    D. implement; inhibit

4. Because the policies of both candidates _____ Dara, she may _____ from voting in the next election.
    A. inhibit; deplete
    B. confound; abstain
    C. inhibit; sustain
    D. confound; prohibit

5. At the sight of an office _____ with medicines and medical instruments, the young country doctor was _____ with delight.
    A. replete; sustained
    B. infused; implemented
    C. infused; confounded
    D. replete; suffused

Exercise IV. Complete the sentence by inferring information about the italicized word from its context.

1. If Muhammad is known to be a *tenacious* fighter, in his upcoming match, he may…

2. If Gloria has decided to *abstain* from smoking, it is likely that…

3. If you *implement* a regular schedule for your homework, you will probably find that…

Exercise V. Fill in the blank with the word from the Unit that best completes the sentence, using the root we supply as a clue. Then, answer the questions that follow the paragraphs.

At the end of World War II, the industrial and military machine that had been Germany lay in ruins. In the 1930s, Germany consisted not only of its present lands, but also of about one-third of present-day Poland, as well as a province near what are now the Baltic states—Latvia, Lithuania, and Estonia. During the war, Adolf Hitler's dream of world domination had brought him about half of France, most of southern and eastern Europe, and parts of the Soviet Union. The determination of the Allies, combined with a lack of supplies, however, had ended the German command. Post-war Germany was a wasteland plagued by looting and rioting, and it had the sort of black market economy found today only in the poorest nations.

Adding to this problem was the German refugee situation. Hitler had claimed that his invasion of Czechoslovakia was prompted by the large German population in the Sudeten region of that country. After the war ended, Czechoslovakia expelled this population—about 12 million citizens of German descent. Poland drove out its citizens of German descent as well.

Germany was also separated into four occupation zones by the victorious Allies: France, Great Britain, the United States, and the Soviet Union. Each of the four Allies was allowed to dismantle factories and take the equipment and raw materials to compensate for the costs of fighting Germany. The Western countries—France, Great Britain, and the United States—did this for only a short time because it quickly became obvious that this process would create starvation and famine for the remaining Germans.

The Soviet Union, however, was more _____ (TEN) in its removal of assets from its part of the former Germany. The desperate poverty of the remaining people in East Germany did little to _____ (HIB) the greed of some of the Soviet victors.

The zones of Germany occupied by the Western allies eventually became West Germany. Under the leadership of its first prime minister, Konrad Adenauer, and with the help of such foreign assistance as the American Marshall Plan, West

Germany quickly rebuilt its economy, and its citizens began to prosper. The Soviet-occupied zone became known as East Germany, and its citizens continued to suffer significant levels of poverty as resources were _____ (PLE) by the Soviet Union. This inequality persisted until the reunification of Germany in 1991. Forty-six years after the end of World War II, a unified Germany was at last given the task of becoming a responsible member of the fellowship of nations.

1.   Which of the following statements is incorrect based on information contained in the second, third, and fourth paragraphs?
     A.   Hitler used the presence of German citizens to justify his invasion of Poland.
     B.   Various countries tried to have no German population after the end of WWII.
     C.   Germany was divided into various occupied zones after the conclusion of WWII.
     D.   Removal of resources from Germany by the Soviet Union stopped shortly after WWII.

2.   According to the passage, the Western Allies stopped removing resources from Germany because
     A.   they realized that the German resources were not profitable.
     B.   they realized that such removal would have a drastic effect on Germany.
     C.   they sold their rights to the resources to the Soviet Union.
     D.   they disliked the idea of importing resources from a former enemy.

3.   Which of the following was NOT a reason for East Germany's poverty after World War II?
     A.   the attempt by the Allies to invade Czechoslovakia
     B.   the expulsion of people of German ancestry from other countries
     C.   the removal of German assets by the victorious nations
     D.   the dismantling of factories

Exercise VI. Drawing on your knowledge of roots and words in context, read the following selection and define the italicized words. If you cannot figure out the meaning of the words on your own, look them up in a dictionary. Note that *de* means "away from" and *pro* means "forth."

The governor called upon National Guard troops last week in an effort to *defuse* the tensions that arose from a dispute between striking factory workers and their replacements. The troops were called in to protect the replacement workers from the violence that had rocked the small town of Manglostone in recent weeks. Following a twelve-hour standoff, the striking workers finally gave way to troops and returned to their more peaceful ways of protesting. Factory owners and local townspeople were *profuse* in their praise of the governor's decision.

UNIT FOUR

FORM
Latin FORMARE, FORMATUM, "to form; to establish"

MISINFORMATION   (mis in fər mā´ shən)   *n.*   untrue or wrong information
L. *mis*, "wrong" + *in*, "in," + *formare* = *wrongly established*
The two warring countries constantly circulated *misinformation* to confuse
each other.

REFORM   (rē fôrm´)   *v.*   to bring back to rightness, order, or morality
L. *re*, "again" + *formare* = *to form again*
Many people think we need to *reform* our political system, but few know where
to start.
syn: correct   *ant: ruin*

FORMATIVE   (fôr´ mə tiv)   *adj.*   occurring at the time of most influence
During a *formative* period of Jay's life, he was introduced to jazz music; now, he is
a famous saxophonist.

APT, EPT
From Latin APTARE, APTUM, "to fit"

INEPT   (in ept´)   *adj.*   unskilled; clumsy
L. *in*, "not" + *aptum* = *not suited*
Try as I might to comfort Alicia, all my words
seemed *inept* or just plain wrong.
syn: awkward   *ant: graceful*

EPPIE the INEPT carpenter realized that she
was APT not to be successful in that line of
work.

ADEPT   (ə dept´)   *adj.*   skilled; expert at
L. *ad*, "toward" + *aptum* = *suited toward*
Tanya was *adept* at dealing with the arguments that often arose on her volleyball
team.
syn: masterful   *ant: incompetent*

APTITUDE   (ap´ ti tōōd)   *n.*   a skill or suitability for
Rob did not discover his *aptitude* for politics until he was in college.
syn: ability

POS, PON
Latin PONERE, POSITUM, "to put; to place"

POSIT   (poz´ it)   *v.*   to put forth; to assert
Tyler *posited* his belief that all people should be treated fairly.
syn: propose

IMPOSE   (im pōz´)   *v.*   to forcibly place upon
L. *in*, "on, onto" + *positum* = *to put onto*
The new government tried to *impose* its ideas onto supporters of the old regime.
syn: inflict

DISPOSITION   (dis pə zish´ ən)   *n.*   one's attitude or mood
L. *dis*, "apart" + *positum*
The pirate captain's murderous *disposition* led him to throw many lazy sailors to the sharks.
syn: character

FIG
Latin FINGERE, FICTUM, "to shape"

FIGMENT   (fig´ mənt)   *n.*   something invented or imaginary
Were the monsters only a *figment* of a feverish brain, or did they really exist?
syn: phantom   *ant: fact*

EFFIGY   (ef´ i jē)   *n.*   a figure constructed in mockery
L. *e*, "out of" + *fictum* = *to shape out of*
An *effigy* of the other team's mascot was burned at the pep rally.

PREFIGURE   (prē fig´ yər)   *v.*   to look like or predict a later thing or event
L. *pre*, "before" + *fictum* = *to shape before*
The small riot outside City Hall *prefigured* a major uprising that occurred later that year.
syn: foreshadow

▣ Dispose *originally meant "to arrange" (literally, "to put things in order apart from one another"). How do you think the word* disposition, *which means "attitude," came from a verb meaning "to arrange"?*

▣ *I have encountered riotous mobs and have been hung in* effigy.
—Susan B. Anthony,
    American suffragette

EXERCISES - UNIT FOUR

Exercise I. Complete the sentence in a way that shows you understand the meaning of the italicized vocabulary word.

1.   In an attempt to *reform* the voting system, the mayor ordered...

2.   Mother was so *adept* at handling multiple tasks that she...

3.   Any attempt to *impose* the no-jaywalking law in this town will lead to...

4.   Zombies are simply unreal; they are just a *figment* of...

5.   Alexander is so *inept* when it comes to cars that...

6.   Whenever I try to *posit* an idea, Denise always...

7.   Josh had an incredible *aptitude* for...

8.   During the *formative* years of Ruth's life, she...

9.   The citizens built an *effigy* of the man because...

10.   A short period of economic decline usually *prefigures* an economic recession because...

11.   Lou's friendly *disposition* prompted Ron to...

12.   The *misinformation* Lydia had received caused her to...

Exercise II. Fill in the blank with the best word from the choices below. One word will not be used.

figment   inept   posit   prefigure   misinformation

1.   The supposedly reliable report turned out to be full of false statistics and _____.

2.   I was pretty _____ as a stagehand; I even lowered the curtain before the play ended.

3.   One _____ of Tyrell's active imagination is his belief that invisible UFOs constantly circle his home.

4.   The medical researcher is going to _____ a bold new idea on a possible cure for cancer.

Fill in the blank with the best word from the choices below. One word will not be used.

impose	aptitude	reform	prefigure	effigy

5. If we want to _____ our legal system, we will first have to face everything that is wrong with it.

6. I have noticed that a small snowstorm often _____ a large one.

7. Try as she might, Elizabeth could not _____ her own will on the other children.

8. Because Troy has a(n) _____ for running, he enjoys track and is one of the best athletes on the team.

Fill in the blank with the best word from the choices below. One word will not be used.

disposition	effigy	formative	impose	adept

9. A(n) _____ handling of the tense situation will result in everyone feeling like a winner.

10. Her natural _____ was gloomy, but she tried not to mope.

11. A(n) _____ of the hated dictator was burned in the town square.

12. I consider the years between 1985 and 1995 to be Joshua's _____ period because he developed all his ideas and opinions then.

Exercise III. Choose the set of words that best completes the sentence.

1. Darnell, who had a natural _____ for science, enjoyed _____ new theories to the other staff in the department.
   A. aptitude; positing
   B. disposition; imposing
   C. aptitude; reforming
   D. disposition; prefiguring

2. Amy's naturally friendly _____ made her _____ at handling social situations.
   A. effigy; adept
   B. aptitude; formative
   C. figment; inept
   D. disposition; adept

3. Rumors and _____ spread by King Paul's enemies finally prompted the crowd to burn a(n) _____ of him in front of the palace.
   A. disposition; figment
   B. misinformation; effigy
   C. aptitude; effigy
   D. figments; disposition

4.   Jeff was not _____ at painting because his hand was injured during a(n) _____ period of his life.
       A. formative; prefigured
       B. adept; reformed
       C. inept; imposed
       D. adept; formative

5.   Carrie believes that rather than _____ harsh sentences on violators of the law, we should try to _____
       criminals and bring them back into society.
       A. reforming; impose
       B. imposing; reform
       C. reforming; posit
       D. positing; impose

Exercise IV. Complete the sentence by inferring information about the italicized word from its context.

1.   If a group of citizens urges the government to *reform* voting laws, it is likely that they believe the laws…

2.   If Frank is an *inept* driver, he probably does things like…

3.   If Nora's *disposition* is unpleasant, the people around her may…

**Exercise V. Fill in the blank with the word from the Unit that best completes the sentence, using the root
     we supply as a clue. Then, answer the questions that follow the paragraphs.**

Although most people have heard of Dracula, the legendary vampire from Transylvania described in Bram Stoker's novel, few know there is an actual, historical basis for the mythic figure. Many scholars believe a man named Prince Vlad was the real Dracula. In 1431, Vlad was born into a noble family of Wallachia, an area close to Transylvania and now part of Romania. Prince Vlad's father, Dracul, was a member of the Order of the Dragon, a group of knights that swore to defend Catholicism against the neighboring Ottoman Turks. The word *dracul* means "dragon" or "devil" in Romanian. Prince Vlad came to be known as Dracula, meaning "son of the dragon or devil." Constant war existed during Prince Vlad's lifetime, largely because the area where he lived bordered on two competing empires, the Turks and the Austrian Habsburgs.

During Prince Vlad's rule, he _____(POS) a totalitarian regime, strengthened the army, and improved trade with neighboring countries. He was an _____ (EPT) military leader who won many famous victories over the Turkish army. The Vatican praised him for defending Christianity, but it soon disapproved of Prince Vlad's infamously cruel methods. He frequently tortured his captured enemies by impaling them on long stakes and leaving them to die in agony. It is rumored that Prince Vlad dined at a table set up among hundreds of impaled men. He was nicknamed Vlad Tepes (meaning "Vlad the Impaler") after his death. It has also been reported that he sometimes ate bread dipped in blood, which scholars _____ (POS) is a probable basis for the myth that he was a vampire. Aside from his grisly deeds in battle, though, Prince Vlad was a strong believer that religious charity would secure his place in heaven. He founded five Catholic monasteries during his reign, and his family continued the tradition, founding fifty more over the next 150 years.

Prince Vlad ruled from 1456 until 1462, when he was defeated and took refuge in Hungary. He briefly regained power in 1476, but he was killed in a battle against the Turkish army, which beheaded his corpse and displayed it at Constantinople. Vlad's remains were later recovered and buried in a monastery near Bucharest called Snagov. In 1931, archaeologists searched this supposed burial site and recovered a casket. The casket contained a skeleton buried with a crown and the ring worn by knights of the Order of the Dragon. Believing they had found Prince Vlad's remains, the archaeologists brought the skeleton to the History Museum in Bucharest. However, the skeleton soon disappeared and has never been found, adding to the mysteries of the legend of Dracula.

1.   What does *Dracula* mean in Romanian?
      A.   vampire
      B.   son of the dragon
      C.   the impaler
      D.   prince

2.   What story may have contributed to the belief that Prince Vlad was a vampire?
      A.   the story that he impaled his enemies
      B.   the belief that he was part of the Order of the Dragon
      C.   the story that he founded monasteries
      D.   the belief that he sometimes ate bread dipped in blood

3.   Where was Prince Vlad supposedly buried?
      A.   Snagov
      B.   Constantinople
      C.   Hungary
      D.   Transylvania

Exercise VI. Drawing on your knowledge of roots and words in context, read the following selection and define the italicized words. If you cannot figure out the meaning of the words on your own, look them up in a dictionary. Note that *pre* means "before, in advance."

Ronni came to school this morning with an imaginative tale of talking sheep on Mars. Her fellow kindergarten classmates loved the story, even though the sheep were simply figments of Ronni's imagination. In fact, their teacher, Mrs. Landings, wasn't surprised at Ronni's storytelling, as she often said that Ronnie had a *predisposition* to fantasy. Much like Mrs. Landings herself, Ronni was naturally drawn to worlds of imagination and dreams.

UNIT FIVE

LEGA
Latin LEGARE, LEGATUM, "to appoint; to send on a mission; to charge with"

LEGACY   (leg´ ə sē)   *n.*   a body of ideas, achievements, and morals; an example
The judge, retiring today, leaves behind a *legacy* of dishonesty and corruption.
syn: heritage

DELEGATE   (del´ ə gāt)   *v.*   to divide up, especially responsibilities
L. *de*, "down" + *legare = to hand down an appointment*
Our parents *delegated* the easiest tasks, like collecting firewood, to the younger children.
syn: designate

ACT, AG
Latin AGERE, ACTUM, "to do, to act"

AGENDA   (a jen´ də)   *n.*   a plan of action; a purpose
L. literally, *those things that must be done*
Although some critics think the author had a political *agenda* in her last novel, she insists that there was no secret purpose.

PROACTIVE   (prō ak´ tiv)   *adj.*   seeking to solve a problem before it occurs
L. *pro*, "before" + *actum = to act before*
Gwen, who was *proactive* about getting a job, was hired right after she graduated from college.

EXACTING   (eg zak´ ting)   *adj.*   demanding perfection; strict
L. *ex*, "out of" + *agere = to drive out of*
The *exacting* conductor sometimes kept the orchestra for hours to practice a single passage.
syn: picky   *ant: lenient*

The customer was so EXACTING that only the EXACT THING satisfied him.

⚜ *We often use the word collegial (con, "with" + legare) to mean "related to a college." In fact, this is its second meaning; its primary definition is "of or related to a colleague." If several people have a collegial relationship, it means they all share power and respect.*

⚜ *In 1961, President John Kennedy announced that it would be America's goal of "landing a man on the moon and returning him safely to the earth" before the end of the decade. Despite his being assassinated in 1963, the United States fulfilled Kennedy's agenda on July 20, 1969.*

PULS, PEL
Latin PELLERE, PULSUM, "to push"

REPULSION   (rē pul´ shən)   *n.*   a desire to avoid; disgust
L. *re*, "back" + *pulsum = a pushing back*
After months of eating primarily peanut butter, Izzie began to feel *repulsion* for it.
syn: horror   *ant: attraction*

DISPEL   (di spel´)   *v.*   to scatter about; to break up
L. *dis*, "apart" + *pellere = to push apart*
Policemen were sent in to *dispel* the crowd of onlookers that had gathered near the accident.
syn: banish   *ant: gather*

PROPEL   (prə pel´)   *v.*   to cause to move toward; to push
L. *pro*, "forward" + *pellere = to push forward*
A strong wind *propelled* the toy boat across the surface of the lake.
syn: push

LAT
Latin LATUM, "brought; carried"

RELATIVE   (rel´ ə tiv)   *adj.*   dependent upon
L. *re*, "back" + *latum = brought back*
The number of people at the beach on any day is *relative* to the weather and the season.

SUPERLATIVE   (sə pûr´ lə tiv)   *adj.*   excellent; above all others
L. *super*, "above" + *latum = carried above*
For *superlative* performance at work, Holly was awarded a big promotion.
syn: superior   *ant: inferior*

DILATE   (dī´ lāt)   *v.*   to widen
L. *dis*, "apart" + *latum = carried apart*
The surgeon *dilated* the opening of Anthony's windpipe so he could breathe better.

Ⅲ *Latum is the fourth principal part of the Latin verb* fero, *which gives us words like* refer, confer, *and* infer.

Ⅲ *Have you ever gone to the eye doctor and had your eyes* dilated? *This procedure involves widening your pupils so that the doctor can see into the back of your eyes.*

EXERCISES - UNIT FIVE

Exercise I. Complete the sentence in a way that shows you understand the meaning of the italicized vocabulary word.

1.   The *legacy* of the courageous athlete was one of hope that…

2.   If I accuse Maria of having a secret *agenda*, it is because…

3.   I was able to *dispel* the rumor by…

4.   The ducks *propelled* themselves along by…

5.   Simon is so *exacting* when it comes to accounting that…

6.   Because my happiness is *relative* to yours,…

7.   Hannah felt extreme *repulsion* when she watched the film because…

8.   Eleanor's academic performance was *superlative* to…

9.   Trixie's pupils were *dilated*, indicating…

10. If Karen really wants to be *proactive* as a salesperson, she should…

11. I decided to *delegate* all the responsibilities because…

Exercise II. Fill in the blank with the best word from the choices below. One word will not be used.

  relative   repulsion   dispel   exacting   superlative

1.   Occasional matches will help your tennis game a little, but only lots of practice will give you _____ skills.

2.   The more _____ Mrs. Logan was with her students, the more careful they became.

3.   If no one tries to _____ a medical myth, people may start to believe it as fact.

4.   My calmness on any given day seems to be _____ to the balance in my bank account.

Fill in the blank with the best word from the choices below. One word will not be used.

| agenda | proactive | repulsion | legacy | delegate |

5.   When Bette saw the sickening mess in her kitchen, she felt nothing but _____.

6.   David sometimes tried to _____ his chores to his younger sisters so he could play baseball with his friends.

7.   I tried to be _____ about the situation and fix the problem before it became truly difficult.

8.   The _____ my grandmother left behind is one of peace and courage.

Fill in the blank with the best word from the choices below. One word will not be used.

| dilate | agenda | propel | proactive |

9.   After making the incision, the surgeon had to _____ the opening even more to have enough room to operate.

10.   The amount of force needed to _____ the car up the hill was more than we could provide by ourselves.

11.   I don't have a hidden _____; I just want to be your friend.

Exercise III. Choose the set of words that best completes the sentence.

1.   The general tried to _____ the sorrows of his troops by praising the _____ of the fallen heroes.
     A.   dilate; repulsion
     B.   dispel; legacy
     C.   propel; agenda
     D.   delegate; legacy

2.   Our boss is so _____ that everything must be perfect before we can move on to a new item on the _____.
     A.   exacting; legacy
     B.   relative; repulsion
     C.   proactive; legacy
     D.   exacting; agenda

3.   Whether the team succeeds or not is _____ to whether the captain _____ some of his authority or keeps it all for himself.
     A.   superlative; dispels
     B.   exacting; propels
     C.   relative; dilates
     D.   relative; delegates

4. Although the movie was called _____ in reviews, some of the more violent scenes prompted _____ in audience members.
   A. exacting; legacy
   B. superlative; repulsion
   C. superlative; agenda
   D. proactive; repulsion

Exercise IV. Complete the sentence by inferring information about the italicized word from its context.

1. If Chef Peter's cooking is said to be *superlative*, the diners in his restaurant will expect that...

2. When Gretchen, who finds reptiles *repulsive*, sees a snake, she will probably...

3. If an Olympic runner is *exacting* with himself, it is probably because he...

Exercise V. Fill in the blank with the word from the Unit that best completes the sentence, using the root we supply as a clue. Then, answer the questions that follow the paragraphs.

Susan B. Anthony worked toward many political goals in her lifetime. In 1849, when she was 29 years old, Anthony became active in the movement to end slavery, which was called "abolitionism." Her family and other anti-slavery Quakers frequently held meetings at their farm about the issue. At about the same time, she also began working to limit the sale of alcohol and included temperance, or avoidance of liquor, as a part of her political _____ (AG). Members of the Temperance Movement believed that drinking alcohol was sinful and had a negative effect on family life. Despite her work on these issues, however, Susan B. Anthony's most important _____ (LEG) is found in the Nineteenth Amendment to the Constitution, which grants women the right to vote.

Ms. Anthony became convinced through her political work with temperance and abolitionism that women must have the right to vote (called "suffrage") in order to influence politics in America. Because of this opinion, in 1869, Susan B. Anthony and Elizabeth Cady Stanton, her lifelong friend and fellow activist, founded the National Woman Suffrage Association to establish the legal right of women to vote. Anthony worked for this cause energetically by touring the country to speak about suffrage. She tried to _____ (PEL) the common idea that a married woman had no need to vote since the husband could express opinions for both of them in elections. Susan B. Anthony spoke before every Congress from 1869 to 1906 to persuade it to pass an amendment granting women their voting rights.

Anthony became president of the National American Woman Suffrage Association in 1892 and continued to promote women's right to vote across the country. Many territories in the newly settled West were granting women suffrage at this time, and Anthony traveled there to ensure those territories would be admitted to the Union with full rights for women. She retired from her position as president in 1900, but continued her political activity internationally, and, in 1904, she presided over the International Council of Women in Berlin.

Anthony died in 1906 at the age of 86, without ever seeing American women win their suffrage rights. In 1920, the Nineteenth Amendment, also known as the Susan B. Anthony Amendment, granting women in the United States the right to vote, was signed into law. Years later, the importance of Susan B. Anthony's work was nationally recognized when her image was chosen for the dollar coin, and in 1979, she became the first woman to be depicted on US currency.

1. What political movements did Susan B. Anthony support, other than women's suffrage?
   A. temperance and religious freedom
   B. temperance and abolitionism
   C. Quakerism and abolitionism
   D. abolitionism and socialism

2. What organization did Susan B. Anthony and Elizabeth Cady Stanton found?
   A. The American Woman Suffrage Association
   B. The National American Woman Suffrage Association
   C. The Union of Woman Suffrage
   D. The National Woman Suffrage Association

3. Susan B. Anthony was the first woman to
   A. speak about women's suffrage.
   B. vote in the West.
   C. have her image appear on US currency.
   D. speak before Congress.

Exercise VI. Drawing on your knowledge of roots and words in context, read the following selection and define the italicized words. If you cannot figure out the meaning of the words on your own, look them up in a dictionary. Note that re means "back" and ex means "out."

After showing up to several team meetings late, the manager was *relegated* to the job of assistant coach. When asked about how he felt regarding his lower position, Assistant Coach Reed said that he was "very upset," and that the move was "unjustified." Team owner Loretta Drake commented that if Reed remained in opposition to the team's policies, the next step would be his *expulsion* from the team. For fans of the Hoover Beavers, though, Reed's firing would cause deep sadness for a former team hero and a local legend.

UNIT SIX

CANT, CHANT
Latin CANERE, CANTUM, "to sing; to call"

RECANT (rē kant´) *v.* to formally withdraw
L. *re*, "back" + *cantum* = *to call back*
Although he was critical of his fellow band members at first, the drummer later *recanted* his disapproval.
syn: repeal   *ant: reaffirm*

INCANTATION (in kan tā´ shən) *n.* a ritual chant
L. *in*, "in" + *cantum* = *to call on (supernatural forces)*
The children, exposed to the words of a foreign language for the first time, thought they were hearing a magical *incantation*.
syn: spell

DISENCHANTED (dis ən chant´ id) *adj.* losing fondness for; disillusioned
The team's fans, who had once loved the star pitcher, grew *disenchanted* with him as he continued to lose game after game.
syn: disappointed   *ant: enthusiastic*

▥ To be enchanted is to be so fascinated or delighted by something that you seem to be under a spell; to be disenchanted is to be unhappy or bored with something, as if the spell has worn off.

AUD
Latin AUDIRE, AUDITUM, "to hear"

INAUDIBLE (in aw´ də bəl) *adj.* so quiet as to be impossible to hear
L. *in*, "not" + *auditum* = *not heard*
Feedback from the microphone grew from an almost *inaudible* buzzing to a deafening shriek.
                    ant: loud

AUDITORY (aw´ dət ôr ē) *adj.* having to do with the sense of hearing
Developing *auditory* skills involves knowing what to listen for and when to listen for it.

AUDIT (aw´ dit) *n.* a thorough review
Once the accounting scandal became public knowledge, an *audit* of the company's finances was called for.

▥ How does the word audit *refer to attending a class in school, but not receiving a grade or credit for it?*

SON
Latin SONARE, SONATUM, "to sound"

DISSONANCE   (dis´ə nəns)   *n.*   unpleasant or unharmonious sound
L. *dis*, "bad" + *sonatum* = *bad sound*
The static blaring from the radio filled the room with a painful *dissonance*.
syn: discord   *ant: harmony*

ASSONANCE   (as´ə nəns)   *n.*   similarity of word sounds, especially vowels
L. *ad*, "near to" + *sonatum* = *sound near to*
The young poet could produce lines of skillful *assonance* and great beauty.

RESONANT   (rez´ə nənt)   *adj.*   having an effect; powerful
L. *re*, "again" + *sonare* = *to sound again*
The music of some composers who died long ago is still *resonant* today.

LOG
Greek LOGEIN, "to speak; to reason"

ANALOGOUS   (ə nal´ə gəs)   *adj.*   comparable to; like
G. *ana*, "according to" + *logein* = *according to reason*
Do you think the invention of the printing press is *analogous* to the invention of
the computer in our own time?
syn: equivalent   *ant: unrelated*

DIALOGUE   (dī´ə log)   *n.*   communication between two or more people
G. *dia*, "between" + *logein* = *to speak between*
The countries had been at war for so long that any kind of *dialogue* seemed
impossible.
syn: conversation

PROLOGUE   (prō´ log)   *n.*   a speech, passage, or event coming before the main
　　　　speech or event
G. *pro*, "before" + *logein* = *to speak before*
In the *prologue* to the novel, the author lists the
main characters and their histories.
syn: preface   *ant: epilogue*

The PRO LOG marched by with the rest of
the LOGS following behind.

Ⅲ *A sonogram is an image produced by ultra-sound—sound waves above 20,000 Hertz, which bounce off a human body and form an image of its interior.*

Ⅲ *Whereas a dialogue is a speech between two or more people, and a prologue is a speech that comes before something, a monologue is a speech by one person.*

EXERCISES - UNIT SIX

Exercise I. Complete the sentence in a way that shows you understand the meaning of the italicized vocabulary word.

1.   The official decided to *recant* his statement because…

2.   Since the actors spoke in *inaudible* whispers, the audience…

3.   The *dissonance* that filled the neighborhood when the band played…

4.   If there were a magical *incantation* for success, almost everyone would…

5.   When I find that a modern situation is *analogous* to a historical one, I wonder if…

6.   Because Cynthia's *auditory* nerve is damaged, she…

7.   Certain great novels are so *resonant* that they…

8.   The little girl became *disenchanted* with the pony ride when…

9.   A careful *audit* of the company's finances was needed because…

10.   If we can establish a *dialogue* between the two groups, then…

11.   Passages of *assonance* in a poem often make a reader…

12.   The *prologue* to the play was intended to…

Exercise II. Fill in the blank with the best word from the choices below. One word will not be used.

incantation   prologue   audit   dialogue   resonant

1.   I thought I'd seen the worst, but this morning was only a(n) _____ to a really bad day.

2.   When the _____ of the bank was completed, the inspector said that everything seemed to be in order.

3.   The bravery of soldiers in World War II is still _____ today.

4.   If you could speak a(n) _____ and turn into something else, what would you be?

Fill in the blank with the best word from the choices below. One word will not be used.

dialogue   analogous   recant   auditory   dissonance

5.   Although Ray likes to tell people he has a(n) _____ problem, the truth is that he just doesn't listen well.

6.   Often, the _____ that results from the baby crying, the dog barking, and the music blaring drives me insane.

7.   This situation is hardly _____ to that one; in fact, they are completely different.

8.   I like to keep a(n) _____ going with my friends; sometimes, we talk all night long.

Fill in the blank with the best word from the choices below. One word will not be used.

audit   recant   assonance   inaudible   disenchanted

9.   I became _____ with living in Peru when the prices for food and clothing started going up.

10.   The combination of words in the song produces a(n) _____ that Hazel finds lovely to hear.

11.   Although his statement was controversial, the governor will not _____.

12.   If you answer the telephone with a(n) _____ mumble, how will I hear you?

Exercise III. Choose the set of words that best completes the sentence.

1.   Whatever the deputy whispered to the Chief of Police was _____ to the audience, but it made the Chief _____ his statement and apologize.
     A.   resonant; audit
     B.   auditory; audit
     C.   inaudible; recant
     D.   analogous; audit

2.   I hardly think Mary's deep unhappiness with her current job is _____ to the times she has been _____ with a job in the past.
     A.   analogous; disenchanted
     B.   analogous; auditory
     C.   resonant; analogous
     D.   inaudible; disenchanted

3.   The noisy city's _____ would create a(n) _____ disturbance for a person with even
       limited hearing ability.
       A.   incantation; inaudible
       B.   dissonance; auditory
       C.   audit; auditory
       D.   dialogue; resonant

4.   A comprehensive _____ of several major power companies led to an open _____
       between consumers and company executives.
       A.   audit; dialogue
       B.   dissonance; audit
       C.   prologue; dissonance
       D.   incantation; dialogue

5.   The words of the _____ were still _____ in my mind long after the play had ended.
       A.   audit; disenchanted
       B.   prologue; resonant
       C.   dissonance; resonant
       D.   audit; disenchanted

Exercise IV. Complete the sentence by inferring information about the italicized word from its context.

1.   When television commercials become a source of *dissonance* to you, then…

2.   Permanent damage to your *auditory* nerves might be caused by…

3.   If your bank undergoes a government *audit*, you might want to…

**Exercise V. Fill in the blank with the word from the Unit that best completes the sentence, using the root
       we supply as a clue. Then, answer the questions that follow the paragraphs.**

On April 4, 1968, civil rights leader Dr. Martin Luther King, Jr. was fatally wounded by a rifle shot that was _____ (SON) for years afterwards. King was visiting Memphis, Tennessee, to support striking sanitation workers. While he was staying at the Hotel Lorraine, Dr. King exited his room to the balcony on his way to dinner. As he paused to speak to someone below, he was struck and killed by a single rifle shot. Authorities arrested James Earl Ray, a white escaped convict, who soon confessed to shooting King from a building across from the hotel. Near the crime scene, investigators found a bag containing a rifle with Ray's fingerprints. Ray was sentenced to life in prison, but he soon _____ (CANT) his admission, claiming his lawyer told him to confess, which would avoid the death penalty. Today, most people believe Ray assassinated King. Yet, a few claim that the assassination was a conspiracy, not carried out solely by James Earl Ray.

Critics who believe in a possible conspiracy cite a number of problems with the official story. Most significantly, Ray was not a trained sniper, nor is there any evidence that he practiced firing rifles on his own. The person who shot Dr. King fired one precision shot. In addition, investigators could never match the bullet from King's body to Ray's rifle, even after new testing was done in 1997. A number of witnesses present at the murder scene claimed the sound of the shot came from the ground, not from above, which is where Ray allegedly fired. A man who had claimed he saw Ray leaving the room later admitted that he was intoxicated. When he was shown a picture, he even denied that Ray was the man he had originally claimed to see. Some people, _____ (CHANT) by the potential problems with the authorities' version of King's assassination, still believe in Ray's possible innocence.

James Earl Ray died in prison in 1998, and Dr. King's family has even publicly stated that they do not believe Ray killed King. In 2000, however, after finishing an eighteen-month investigation, the Justice Department concluded that there was no evidence of an assassination plot. Today, the official story remains unaltered from the original—that James Earl Ray, and only James Earl Ray, was responsible for killing Martin Luther King, Jr.

1. Where was Dr. Martin Luther King, Jr. assassinated?
   A. the Hotel Lorraine
   B. a boarding house
   C. the Holiday Inn
   D. a Memphis courtroom

2. Why do some people believe that James Earl Ray is innocent?
   A. His fingerprints were not found on a rifle near the crime scene.
   B. He was somewhere else at the time of the shooting.
   C. He was not a trained sniper.
   D. He had no reason to kill King.

3. The author of the passage presents
   A. all the known facts about the assassination of Martin Luther King, Jr.
   B. the assassination and what happened afterwards chronologically.
   C. James Earl Ray not as the killer, but as part of a larger conspiracy.
   D. various facts of Ray's behavior in the days before the assassination

Exercise VI. Drawing on your knowledge of roots and words in context, read the following selection and define the italicized words. If you cannot figure out the meaning of the words on your own, look them up in a dictionary. Note that *epi* means "after" and *eu* means "good."

Although it has been more than sixty years since it first opened on Broadway, Arthur Miller's tragedy *Death of A Salesman* still has audiences weeping during its *epilogue*. The closing speech by Willy's wife Linda is a touching and heartfelt *eulogy* for her recently deceased husband. If it is done well, the farewell monologue can be amazingly powerful.

UNIT SEVEN

BELL
Latin BELLUM, "war"

BELLICOSE (bel´ i kōs) *adj.* warlike in nature
The *bellicose* tribe was in the habit of fighting its neighbors.
syn: combative   *ant:* peaceful

ANTEBELLUM (an tē bel´ əm) *adj.* occurring before a war
L. *ante,* "before" + *bellum* = *before the war*
War changed the country in many ways, but some things remained as they were in the *antebellum* years.

BELLIGERENCE (bə lij´ ər əns) *n.* a warlike mood or attitude
L. *bellum* + *gero,* "to wage" = *waging war*
Despite the *belligerence* of the opposing team, the Hawks won the game by two points.
                    ant: peace

> ⚖ *The word* antebellum *often describes something set or created in the southern United States before the Civil War.*

AM
Latin AMOR, "love"
Latin AMICUS, "friend"

ENAMORED (e nam´ ərd) *adj.* fond of; feeling love toward
L. *in,* "in" + *amor* = *in love*
At first, I hated the novel, but after reading it again, I became *enamored* of it.
syn: charmed   *ant:* repulsed

AMIABLE (ā´ mē ə bəl) *adj.* good-natured; cheerful
Bernard greeted me with an *amiable* smile as I entered the office.
syn: cordial   *ant:* disagreeable

AMICABLE (am´ i kə bəl) *adj.* not bitter or hostile; friendly
There were rumors that Diana and Brynn were fighting, but the two girls insisted they had an *amicable* relationship.

> ⚖ *An* amicus curiae, *or "friend of the court," is a person or group that offers advice on legal cases to a judge.*

AMICABLE AMY'S friendly manner did not impress the alligators.

AGON
Greek AGON, "contest; struggle"

ANTAGONIZE   (an tag´ ə nīz)   *v.*   to act hostile toward; to provoke
G. *anti*, "against" + *agon* = *to struggle against*
No matter how the bullies *antagonize* Walter, he never gets angry or upset.
syn: oppose   *ant: soothe*

PROTAGONIST   (prō tag´ ə nist)   *n.*   the central character in a work of literature
G. *proto*, "first" + *agon* = *first contestant*
In the first story Jo wrote, the *protagonist* was a princess who defeated a wicked emperor.

ANTAGONIST   (an tag´ ə nist)   *n.*   one who is hostile toward; one who opposes
G. *anti*, "against" + *agon* = *contestant who is against*
Ann sometimes felt like her parents were her *antagonists*, but at other times, they seemed like her best friends.

PHIL
Greek PHILE, "love"

PHILOSOPHICAL   (fil ə säf´ i kəl)   *adj.*   calm and wise; reasonable
G. *phile* + *sophos*, "wisdom" = *love of wisdom*
Cheryl's friends thought she would be humiliated after she lost the contest, but she was *philosophical* about the whole thing.

PHILANTHROPY   (fi lan´ thrə pē)   *n.*   charitable donation to public causes
G. *phile* + *anthropos*, "man" = *love of man*
The farmer gave his land to the city to turn into a park and was praised for his act of *philanthropy*.
                    ant: stinginess

BIBLIOPHILE   (bib´ lē ə fīl)   *n.*   one who loves books
G. *biblios*, "book" + *phile* = *love of books*
Cameron, a self-described *bibliophile*, was running out of space for her books.

> Greek drama usually has a struggle or contest (agon) at its center. The protagonist is the main figure in such a drama, and the antagonist is the figure who opposes the protagonist.

> The Greek word for "brother" is adelphos; what does Philadelphia literally mean?

EXERCISES - UNIT SEVEN

Exercise I. Complete the sentence in a way that shows you understand the meaning of the italicized vocabulary word.

1.   We knew the brothers were *bellicose* because…

2.   Since Lili is not *enamored* of the summer weather,…

3.   Wally found that the best way to *antagonize* his brother was to…

4.   The economy began to improve after the war, even though in the *antebellum* period, it…

5.   Do you identify with the *protagonist* of the novel, or are you more like…

6.   Although their lives grew apart, the two friends had an *amicable* relationship because…

7.   If I were a multimillionaire, I would definitely engage in *philanthropy* because…

8.   The *belligerence* Jack felt was clear when…

9.   Eric's little sister seemed like his *antagonist* when she…

10. Because Bud was *amiable* by nature, the people around him…

11. A true *bibliophile* can be identified by…

12. Parker had a *philosophical* outlook about his life's hardships, which made him seem…

Exercise II. Fill in the blank with the best word from the choices below. One word will not be used.

belligerence	amicable	antagonist	protagonist	bibliophile

1.   The two countries remained on _____ terms despite an incident many feared would hurt diplomatic relations.

2.   When interviewing for a job, it is best to show assertiveness, but not _____.

3.   The lion is a natural _____ to the zebra.

4.   Hank used to go to parties often, but now, he's a(n) _____ who would rather stay home with a book.

Fill in the blank with the best word from the choices below. One word will not be used.

antagonize   protagonist   belligerent   amiable   philanthropy

5.   The donation of the library was part of a generous act of _____ by the town's wealthiest widow.

6.   While Thelma did not get along well with others, her brother Devon was _____ and easygoing.

7.   It is hard to identify the _____ in a novel with so many important characters.

8.   If you _____ that cat, don't be surprised when she scratches you.

Fill in the blank with the best word from the choices below. One word will not be used.

antebellum   amiable   philosophical   enamored   bellicose

9.   If I get some perspective on my life, perhaps I can be a little more _____.

10. In the _____ South, the tensions that would lead to war were building.

11. Ralph was so _____ of the kite that he took it out even when there was no breeze.

12. If Leo keeps directing _____ comments at his mom, he is destined for trouble.

Exercise III. Choose the set of words that best completes the sentence.

1.   The football team is full of _____ players, who are always _____ toward the opposing team and start fights with them.
     A.   philosophical; antagonistic
     B.   bellicose; antagonistic
     C.   bellicose; amicable
     D.   amiable; belligerent

2.   The actor portraying the _____ of the play was _____ of his female lead both on and off the stage.
     A.   protagonist; philosophical
     B.   antagonist; amicable
     C.   antagonist; amiable
     D.   protagonist; enamored

3.   Harry believed that his wealthy parents should put more money toward _____ and often acted as his father's _____ in family arguments on the subject.
     A.   philanthropy; antagonist
     B.   protagonists; belligerence
     C.   philanthropy; bibliophile
     D.   bibliophiles; protagonist

4. Despite Rodney's _____ attitude at first, he and Fran went on to develop a(n) _____ partnership.
    A. philosophical; bellicose
    B. belligerent; amicable
    C. amicable; philosophical
    D. antebellum; bellicose

5. The bookstore café was a natural gathering spot for _____, who would greet one another in a(n) _____ fashion and then settle down to their individual reading.
    A. protagonists; bellicose
    B. bibliophiles; amiable
    C. bibliophiles; enamored
    D. antagonists; amicable

Exercise IV. Complete the sentence by inferring information about the italicized word from its context.

1. If Noreen *antagonizes* her fellow students, they may decide to…

2. Some of the signs that your new manager is of a *belligerent* nature might include…

3. If the reading public is *enamored* of a new author, the author's books will probably…

Exercise V. Fill in each blank with the word from the Unit that best completes the sentence, using the root we supply as a clue. Then, answer the questions that follow the paragraphs.

Although most people know that Thomas Jefferson was the third president of the United States and the author of the Declaration of Independence, they may not realize that he was also a well-respected intellectual. Jefferson was recognized worldwide for his knowledge of mathematics and science. In fact, he was so _____ (AM) of science that he carried various scientific instruments, as well as a small notebook, in his pockets at all times. Every day, no matter where he traveled in the world, Jefferson would take time to observe the weather, the animals, and the plants around him. He recorded all of these observations in his pocket notebook.

Thomas Jefferson also loved to read about science, and he was able to read in seven different languages. He was a dedicated _____ (PHIL) who kept thousands of books at his home. He kept books handy throughout his house so that he could read any time that he had a few minutes free. If he read in the evening, Jefferson would often become so involved in a book that he would get up early the next day to read more of it.

Some historians believe that Thomas Jefferson's love of science led him to create one of the major accomplish-ments of his presidency: the Lewis and Clark Expedition. There had been no complete study of the western United States when Jefferson became president in 1801. For only $2,500, he funded the Lewis and Clark Expedition, whose main purpose was to find a trade route to the Pacific Ocean; he instructed the leaders of the group, Meriwether Lewis and William Clark, to keep detailed journals and notes of all of the different plants and animals they saw on their journey. He also asked them to bring back samples of seeds and plants they found along the way. These were planted at his home, an _____ (BELL) mansion in Virginia called Monticello. Jefferson himself carefully monitored the plants' progress, kept records of their growth, and experimented with crossbreeding them.

After he left the presidency, Jefferson retired to Monticello. From there, he wrote letters to scientists all over the world. He often requested plants or seed samples from foreign countries. When these samples were sent to him, Jefferson would carefully plant them in grids he designed so that he could scientifically monitor the growth of the plants. The descendants of many of these plants are still being grown at Monticello, which is now a historical site.

1. Which of the following would be the best title for this passage?
    A. Thomas Jefferson: An American Politician
    B. American Patriots
    C. The Man Who Wrote the Declaration of Independence
    D. The Scientific Pursuits of Thomas Jefferson

2. According to this passage, which of the following was the main reason for the Lewis and Clark Expedition?
    A. to learn about various Native American cultures
    B. to record observations about plant and animal life in the western United States
    C. to find a trade route to the Pacific Ocean
    D. to collect plant samples from the western states

3. Why did Thomas Jefferson want plant and seed samples from around the world sent to Monticello?
    A. so he could create a beautiful garden
    B. because he was drafting agricultural laws
    C. so he could plant them and monitor their growth himself
    D. to keep the plants alive for the future

4. Thomas Jefferson's contribution to science remains today in
    A. his love of reading.
    B. his letters to other scientists.
    C. his scientific instruments.
    D. the plants and seeds still being grown at Monticello.

Exercise VI. Drawing on your knowledge of roots and words in context, read the following selection and define the italicized words. If you cannot figure out the meaning of the words on your own, look them up in a dictionary. Note that *post* means "after," and *mis* means "against."

The years following the American Civil War constitute the period known as Reconstruction. In this *postbellum* society, the South tried to rebuild with the help and support of the North. By giving money, supplies, and time, Northern donors acted in a most generous and truly American way and helped defuse the *misanthropic* spirit that had divided so many families and communities.

UNIT EIGHT

PED
Latin PES, PEDIS, "foot"

IMPEDIMENT   (im ped´ ə mənt)   *n.*   something that gets in the way; an obstacle
L. *in*, "in the way of" + *pedis* = *in the way of the foot*
One mistake at work need not be an *impediment* to your advancement in the company.
syn: barrier   *ant: assistance*

EXPEDIENT   (ek spē´ dē ənt)   *adj.*   practical; prudent
L. *ex*, "by" + *pedis* = *(to speed along) by foot*
Jasper decided it would be most *expedient* for him to leave town as soon as he could.
syn: profitable

PEDESTRIAN   (pə dəs´ trē ən)   *adj.*   lacking excitement; ordinary and dull
Although I thought my trip to the city would be thrilling, it turned out to be rather *pedestrian*.
syn: everyday   *ant: original*

PED
Greek PAIS, PAIDOS, "child"

PEDANT   (ped´ ənt)   *n.*   one possessing abundant knowledge of minor, often uninteresting, things
Only a *pedant* would go into such detail on the most minor points of grammar.

PEDAGOGUE   (ped´ ə gäg)   *n.*   a teacher, especially one who is dull and narrow minded
G. *paidos* + *agein*, "to lead" = *child-leader*
Because our previous teacher had been a terrible bore, we expected the new teacher to be a *pedagogue* of the same type.

▥ Pedestrian *literally means "going on foot" and once referred to writing that plodded dully along rather than moving gracefully and with art. Today, anything that is dull or commonplace can be called* pedestrian.

▥ *Words from Latin* pedis *and Greek* paidos *are easy to mix up. One clue: if you see* ped *spelled* paed, *it is from* paidos.

VEST

Latin VESTIS, "clothing"

TRAVESTY   (trav´ əs tē)   *n.*   a bad imitation of; a perversion of
Some of the books being published today are a *travesty* of the great literature that came before them.
syn: mockery, farce   *ant: glorification*

VESTED   (ves´ təd)   *adj.*   significant to one's own profit or well-being
Because Joy does not have a *vested* interest in the company, she doesn't have to worry if it goes bankrupt.

VESTMENT   (vest´ mənt)   *n.*   clothing worn to symbolize religious or political authority
The youngest members of the choir did not want to wear their *vestments* because they felt that the clothes weren't cool.

DIVEST   (dī vest´)   *v.*   to strip or remove a title or position of authority
L. *dis*, "apart" + *vestis* = *to remove clothing*
When his cheating was discovered, Brian was *divested* of the office of student body president.
                    ant: endow

CORPOR, CORPU

Latin CORPOR, "body"

CORPOREAL   (kôr pôr´ ē əl)   *adj.*   having to do with the body
Some religious writers focus on the differences between *corporeal* form and spiritual essence.

CORPULENT   (kôr´ pyi lənt)   *adj.*   extremely fat; obese
L. *corpor* + *-ulent*, "full" = *full of body*
It seems shameful that the king is *corpulent* while his people are thin and starving.
                    ant: skinny

The two sergeants could not lift the CORPULENT CORPORAL.

INCORPORATE   (in kôr´ pər āt)   *v.*   to bring together features, ideas, or elements
L. *in*, "into" + *corpor* = *into a body*
The most popular recipes in the cookbook manage to *incorporate* ideas about health and nutrition without sacrificing flavor.
syn: include, join   *ant: separate, remove*

▥ A travesty is *a form of drama that ridicules something or someone. The players in the drama sometimes wear ridiculous-looking clothing. Outside of the theater, a travesty is a gross mockery or perversion of something.*

▥ Other words from corpor: corps, corpse, corporation, corpuscle, corporeal, incorporate, corpulent.

EXERCISES - UNIT EIGHT

Exercise I. Complete the sentence in a way that shows you understand the meaning of the italicized vocabulary word.

1. Fear can be an *impediment* to success if you…

2. I believe that the trial was a *travesty* of justice, simply…

3. Those who believe in an afterlife feel that a person's *corporeal* form…

4. Although Travis knows a lot, he never seems like a *pedant* because…

5. Because I have a *vested* interest in the outcome of this horse race,…

6. A doctor may advise an extremely *corpulent* patient to…

7. The *vestments* worn by the priest are a symbol of…

8. The beauty queen was *divested* of her crown after she…

9. When Rudy said my life seemed *pedestrian*, I argued that…

10. Politicians tend to select the most *expedient*…

11. The substitute deserved his reputation as a *pedagogue* because…

12. This type of exercise *incorporates* many forms in order to…

Exercise II. Fill in the blank with the best word from the choices below. One word will not be used.

pedant	vestment	divest	corporeal	corpulent

1. After the scandal rocked the company, the vice president was _____ of his authority.

2. I lectured my friends a little too long on minor points today; now, I'm afraid they think I'm a
   _____.

3. When the dog became so _____ that he could hardly get through the pet door, Ernest knew it was time to put him on a diet.

4. Simply donning the _____ of a judge does not make a person sure to hand out wise or fair decisions.

Fill in the blank with the best word from the choices below. One word will not be used.

pedestrian   travesty   pedant   corporeal   impediment

5.   One of the biggest _____ to successful weight loss is the constant stream of food commercials on TV.

6.   When I learned of the imprisonment of an innocent man, I felt I was living in a(n) _____ of democracy.

7.   My _____ form is slightly short, but I make up for it by having a generous spirit.

8.   While Ellie thought Joe's taste in music was a little _____, he thought her music was bizarre.

Fill in the blank with the best word from the choices below. One word will not be used.

corpulent   vested   pedagogue   incorporate   expedient

9.   Everyone on the team has a(n) _____ stake in how the season plays out.

10.   If we _____ some of today's ideas into the earlier plan, I feel certain we will succeed.

11.   Barry thinks it will be most _____ to buy the cell phone at full price now and try to be reimbursed by the company later.

12.   I thought the visiting speaker would be a boring _____, but his speech was actually short and fascinating.

Exercise III. Choose the set of words that best completes the sentence.

1.   Rather than considering the different backgrounds of your teammates a(n) _____, try to _____ diversity into your overall strategy.
     A.   impediment; incorporate
     B.   travesty; divest
     C.   pedagogue; incorporate
     D.   pendant; divest

2.   After he was _____ his position at the university, Karl obtained a position at the local high school, where he spent the rest of his career as a boring _____.
     A.   incorporated; pedant
     B.   divested; pedagogue
     C.   incorporated; impediment
     D.   divested; travesty

3.   The lazy, _____ emperor, who spent far more time at banquets than at political negotiations, represented a(n) _____ all the noble ideals held by previous rulers.
      A. corporeal; impediment
      B. pedestrian; pedagogue
      C. corpulent; travesty
      D. vested; vestment

4.   Despite the famous author's fascinating _____ presence in the room, his speaking style was disappointingly _____.
      A. corpulent; expedient
      B. expedient; corporeal
      C. corporeal; pedestrian
      D. pedestrian; vested

5.   Because we didn't have a(n) _____ interest in the subject, the man talking endlessly about it seemed a terrible _____.
      A. expedient; pedestrian
      B. corporeal; pedant
      C. vested; pedant
      D. corpulent; pedagogue

Exercise IV. Complete the sentence by inferring information about the italicized word from its context.

1.   If Lou tells Penny that the meals at the restaurant are *pedestrian*, Penny will probably…

2.   Tamara said that taking a job in another city is the most *expedient* option for her; we might, therefore, assume that she will…

3.   If Ron is *divested* of his authority in the company, we can assume that he…

Exercise V. Fill in the blank with the word from the Unit that best completes the sentence, using the root we supply as a clue. Then, answer the questions that follow the paragraphs.

It is nearly impossible to walk down the hallways of an American public school without seeing glowing lights surrounded by excited students, especially around lunchtime. These lights point the way to a solution for school funding, or they become places where a _____ (CORPU) generation can ruin its health. These lights, of course, come from soda, snack, and ice cream machines. They may indeed provide money for student activities, hallway video cameras, even metal detectors, but they create poor eating habits, feed caffeine addictions, and raise student consumption of sugar and salt far above recommended levels.

Study after study demonstrates that Americans are becoming increasingly overweight. Diabetes is appearing in younger and younger children, and people are gaining weight at faster and faster rates. People tend to establish their habits for living during childhood; at this point in time, though, many children do not lead healthy lifestyles. Children in earlier generations spent much of their time playing games of endurance, running around, or exploring on bicycles, but children in our own time are more likely to be captivated by video games or television after school. This lack of activity can have dramatic effects.

Over thirty years ago, soda machines contained twelve-ounce cans; now, they contain twenty-ounce bottles. This 75% increase in volume is part of a huge increase in obesity and related health risks. When soda machines are presented as an option for students after every class period, the health of our future generations is placed in danger. This reckless behavior by school principals and superintendents is a _____ (VEST) of responsible supervision.

Beyond any doubt, the revenues from soda machines and snack machines have given schools an additional source of funding without raising taxes. However, many students are not responsible enough to make healthy choices about the things that they eat and drink. In addition, school administrators may not have thought about the way that the chemicals they are selling will affect student behavior and performance. The idea of vending machines is a good one; the snacks, drinks, and junk food that currently lurk inside these machines, however, need to be eliminated.

1.   Why does the author mention metal detectors?
      A.   as a way of explaining what the essay will be about
      B.   to acknowledge that snack machines have some benefit
      C.   to show the opinions of school administrators
      D.   as an explanation of dangers to future generations

2.   Which of the following may NOT be concluded from the second paragraph?
      A.   Children today are not as active as children in previous generations were.
      B.   Appetites have increased in the past thirty years.
      C.   Increased levels of technology have reduced the physical activity of children.
      D.   Childhood activity has an influence on adult behavior.

3.   What does the author specifically say is being done with vending machines?
      A.   They are being completely eliminated.
      B.   They hold larger containers of soda than in the past.
      C.   They are places for students to congregate.
      D.   They generate money for school funding.

Exercise VI. Drawing on your knowledge of roots and words in context, read the following selection and define the italicized words. If you cannot figure out the meaning of the words on your own, look them up in a dictionary. Note that *ex* means "out of."

The principal of the school became concerned when several parents approached him with allegations of *corporal* punishment by his teachers. He quickly decided that a workshop was needed to remedy this problem of physical punishment. The school board *expedited* the approval process for the workshop by granting money immediately.

UNIT NINE

UNI
Latin UNUS, "one"

UNIFORM   (yōō′ nə fôrm)   *adj.*   the same all the way through; consistent
L. *unus + formis*, "form" = *one form*
If you bake the cake properly, it will be of *uniform* sweetness and moistness.
syn: unvarying   *ant: variable, disparate*

UNISON   (yōō′ nə sən)   *n.*   one voice
L. *unus + sonus*, "sound" = *one sound*
When the speaker asked the people to answer him, they shouted back in *unison*.

UNANIMOUS   (yōō nan′ ə məs)   *adj.*   showing complete agreement
L. *unus + animus*, "spirit" = *one spirit*
Many trials are dragged out over a long period of time because the jury cannot come to a *unanimous* decision.
syn: harmonious   *ant: divided*

> ⫿ *I probably believe that the worth opinions in the court have been* unanimous *because there's nobody on the other side pointing out all the flaws.*
> —Antonin Scalia,
> US Supreme Court Justice

MONO
Greek MONOS, "one"

MONOLOGUE   (män′ ə lôg)   *n.*   a speech made by a single person
G. *monos + logein*, "to speak" = *a speech by one*
A messenger interrupts the hero of the novel in the middle of a *monologue*.

TWO LOGS speaking is a dialogue; ONE LOG speaking is a MONOLOGUE.

MONOPOLIZE   (mə näp′ ə līz)   *v.*   to use or take so as to prevent others from using or taking
G. *monos + polein*, "sell," = *one seller*
Quentin is *monopolizing* the copy machine, and no one else can use it.
syn: hoard   *ant: share*

MONOGAMY   (mə nog′ ə mē)   *n.*   marriage to only one person at a time
G. *monos + gamy*, "marry" = *marry one*
While multiple marriages are acceptable and even encouraged in some countries, American society generally insists on *monogamy*.

> ⫿ *A* monolith *was originally a huge block or column of only one kind of stone; today,* monolithic *can describe anything that is completely the same throughout.*

MONOLITHIC   (män ə lith′ ik)   *adj.*   exactly the same throughout; lacking any diversity
G. *monos + lithos*, "stone" = *one stone*
Marcie escaped the *monolithic* society she had grown up in by traveling the world and seeing many different cultures.
syn: invariable

HOMO
Greek HOMOS, "the same"

HOMONYM (häm´ ə nim) *n.* a word spelled exactly like another word, but having a different meaning
G. *homos,* + *onym,* "name" = *the same name*
When you come across a *homonym,* like the word *bear,* you may have difficulty figuring out which meaning to assign to it.

HOMOGENIZED (hə mäj´ ə nīzd) *adj.* forced to be exactly the same
G. *homos* + *genos,* "kind" = *the same kind*
Mrs. Benau does not support a *homogenized* class; she thinks all students have different strengths and weaknesses.
ant: diverse

EQUI
Latin AEQUUS, "equal, even"

EQUITABLE (ek´ wit ə bəl) *adj.* fair; just
Zachary usually tried to be *equitable,* but this time, he took all the money for himself and left none for his friend.
syn: balanced   *ant: unjust*

EQUILIBRIUM (ē kwi lib´ rē əm) *n.* balance; steadiness
L. *aequus* + *libra,* "scales, balance" = *equal balance*
Wendy's hurtful comment upset my mental *equilibrium,* and I did badly on my final exam.
syn: evenness

INIQUITY (in ik´ wə tē) *n.* an injustice; a wrong or wicked action or situation
L. *in,* "not" + *aequus* = *not equal*
The city committed a great *iniquity* against local children when it permanently closed the school.
syn: corruption   *ant: morality*

III A homophone (homos, "same" + phonos, "sound") is a word pronounced exactly like another word, but spelled differently and having a different meaning. For example, bear is a homophone *for* bare.

III A mathematical equation *is a statement that makes two expressions* equal, *or* aequus. *One of the most famous* equations *is Einstein's* $E=MC^2$.

EXERCISES - UNIT NINE

Exercise I. Complete the sentence in a way that shows you understand the meaning of the italicized vocabulary word.

1.   The fog was of *uniform* thickness, so no matter where we walked,...

2.   The children found it difficult to sing in *unison* because...

3.   My talks with Lisa always seem to turn into a *monologue* on her part, and...

4.   *Homonyms* in English sound...

5.   They could not come to an *equitable* agreement about the pie because...

6.   The motion to fine people who litter received a *unanimous* vote because...

7.   When my sister began to *monopolize* the car we share,...

8.   If you feel that your emotional *equilibrium* has been upset, try...

9.   If we look closely, we can see that our society is not *monolithic*, but it is...

10. The preacher said that modern society will descend into *iniquity* if...

11. *Monogamy* in most animals is rare, but among humans,...

12. One recent development that has resulted in a more *homogenized* culture is...

Exercise II. Fill in the blank with the best word from the choices below. One word will not be used.

   monolithic   iniquity   monologue   homonym   unanimous

1.   In such a(n) _____ society, it is hard to find many different viewpoints.

2.   New learners of English often have trouble distinguishing between _____.

3.   Although the legal system created terrible _____, it was still possible to get a fair trial.

4.   The family tried repeatedly, but they could not come to a(n) _____ decision on politics.

Fill in the blank with the best word from the choices below. One word will not be used.

unison   monogamy   equitable   homonym   monologue

5.   Do you think _____ requires that married people remain truly in love with one another?

6.   When the teacher greeted her students, they all answered her in _____.

7.   The long _____ delivered by Hamlet in Act III is my favorite part of the play.

8.   The deal, which had seemed _____ to Damien, started to seem less fair as he counted his money.

Fill in the blank with the best word from the choices below. One word will not be used.

homogenized   uniform   equilibrium   monopolize   iniquity

9.   For a magic instant, the twins on the seesaw achieved a perfect _____.

10. Danny always _____ the phone so that no one else in the family could get close to it.

11. My neighborhood seemed _____ and boring to me until I started to ask people about where they had come from.

12. The restaurant's dress code was _____ with that of every other establishment on the boulevard.

Exercise III. Choose the set of words that best completes the sentence.

1.   The Buddhist monk spoke on the difficulty of achieving spiritual _____ in a world filled with _____.
     A. unison; monologues
     B. equilibrium; iniquity
     C. unison; equilibrium
     D. equilibrium; homonyms

2.   A(n) _____ distribution of resources cannot be achieved if one country insists on _____ the world markets.
     A. unanimous; monopolizing
     B. monolithic; homogenizing
     C. uniform; homogenizing
     D. equitable; monopolizing

3.   The play begins with the protagonist's _____; when he finishes, the Chorus enters, speaking together in _____.
     A. iniquity; homonym
     B. monologue; unison
     C. equilibrium; uniform
     D. monologue; iniquity

4.   Because the Senate is practically _____ this year, it comes as no surprise that so many bills pass by _____ approval.
      A.   equitable; uniform
      B.   unanimous; homonym
      C.   monolithic; unanimous
      D.   equitable; uniform

5.   Many fear that our society, which is not _____ by nature, is being forcibly _____ by mass commercialization.
      A.   unanimous; monopolized
      B.   uniform; homogenized
      C.   uniform; monolithic
      D.   equitable; homogenized

Exercise IV. Complete the sentence by inferring information about the italicized word from its context.

1.   If a candidate for the school board calls for a more *equitable* distribution of school funds, we can assume he believes that…

2.   If five friends are *unanimous* in their desire to go to the zoo, they will probably make plans to…

3.   If a character is in the middle of a *monologue*, we can assume the other characters are…

Exercise V. Fill in the blank with the word from the Unit that best completes the sentence, using the root we supply as a clue. Then, answer the questions that follow the paragraphs.

Some people consider religion a negative force in their lives. While this opinion is not _____ (UNI), many people subscribe to it; they say that more people have died in the name of religion over the years than for any other reason. This may or may not be true; the various factions fighting for _____ (EQUI) treatment in societies around the world feel that the injustices they are called on to endure warrant the action they take.

Each of us believes in something: It may be life after death; it may be treating Mother Earth with respect; it may be readiness for salvation. Regardless of what we hear preached from the pulpit, coming from our parents, or rising from the depths of our consciousness, religion has played a very large role in the shaping of the world as we know it. However, one religion does not _____ (MONO) all cultures on Earth. It is the interaction of human beings, pursuing their happiness in whatever way they see fit, that makes the world an interesting place.

You can be a Christian, Muslim, Jew, Buddhist, Confucian, or animist; it really doesn't matter. Each of us must live according to our conscience as we seek peace on Earth. Religion may not be the answer to all of our problems, but life on Earth is certainly interesting because of the idea of religion.

What if you're not religious? Some young people pride themselves on being "without religion." That's certainly another acceptable view. But, when the chips are down, when everything seems to be going wrong, when there is another crisis in the world which seems closer to home, it can help to have a religious belief. It helps to be able to find a force bigger than you are to appeal to in an effort to keep the world from slipping further into chaos. That's when religion comes in handy. When you are confronted with problems that are bigger than you are, religion gives you a way to deal with them.

1.   According to the author, what role does religion play when problems seem overwhelming in the world?
      A.   It plays no role.
      B.   It plays an essential role.
      C.   It gives you a way to deal with problems.
      D.   The role is up to the individual.

2.   According to the article, who believes religion is the root of our problems?
      A.   everyone
      B.   some people
      C.   nobody
      D.   politicians

3.   The author clearly believes religion is
      A.   all-important.
      B.   somewhat important.
      C.   not important at all.
      D.   of unknown importance.

Exercise VI. Drawing on your knowledge of roots and words in context, read the following selection and define the italicized words. If you cannot figure out the meaning of the words on your own, look them up in a dictionary. Note that *an* means "not," and *valent* means "having force."

A penguin is an *anomaly* among birds. Unlike most other birds, penguins have wings but cannot fly. They can swim and feed underwater. They also differ in mating style, since they choose a mate for life. The behavior of male penguins as they court is *equivalent* to a human marriage proposal.

UNIT TEN

BEN
Latin BENE, "well, good"

BENEVOLENT (bə nev´ ə lənt) *adj.* kindly; favorable toward
L. *bene* + *volere*, "to wish" = *to wish well*
A *benevolent* neighbor put the runaway boy up for the night.
syn: humane   *ant: cold-hearted*

BENEFACTOR (ben´ ə fak tər) *n.* a person who gives friendly aid
L. *bene* + *facere*, "to do" = *one who does good*
When the artist began to paint in a strange, new style, her usual *benefactor* withdrew all financial support.

BENIGN (bə nīn´) *adj.* causing no harm
Although police initially thought the substance was a deadly chemical, they soon discovered it was totally *benign*.
ant: deadly

Ben's NINE BENIGN poodles made poor guard dogs.

CORD
Latin COR, CORDIS, "heart"

ACCORD (ə kôrd´) *n.* a sameness of opinion; agreement
L. *ad*, "near to" + *cordis* = *heart toward*
The leaders of the nation were in *accord* on the necessity of a new budget, but no one could agree on how the money should be spent.
syn: harmony   *ant: strife*

DISCORD (dis´ kôrd) *n.* a lack of agreement; disharmony
L. *dis*, "apart" + *cordis* = *heart apart from*
Although they tried to hide their disagreement, the *discord* between the two teammates was obvious.
syn: disunity

CORDIAL (kôr´ djəl) *adj.* warmly friendly and polite
If Leon can't be *cordial* toward his ex-girlfriend, he shouldn't go to her party.
syn: courteous   *ant: hostile*

ANIM
Latin ANIMUS, "spirit"

ANIMOSITY   (an ə mäs´ ə tē)   *n.*   anger or hostility
Despite all the insults he had received, Aaron expressed no *animosity* toward anyone.
syn: bitterness   *ant: civility*

EQUANIMITY   (ek wə nim´ ə tē)   *n.*   an evenness of mind or spirit; calm
L. *aequus*, "even" + *animus* = *even-spirited*
After her father reassured her, the small girl was able to face the bully with *equanimity*.
syn: composure   *ant: hysteria*

MAGNANIMOUS   (mag nan´ ə məs)   *adj.*   generous in spirit
L. *magnus*, "large" + *animus* = *great-spirited*
It was quite *magnanimous* of Stewart to shake hands with Neil, even after Neil tried to trip him at the track meet.
syn: unselfish   *ant: greedy*

MAL
Latin MALUS, "bad"

DISMAL   (diz´ məl)   *adj.*   causing great sadness or negativity
L. *dies*, "day" + *malus* = *evil day*
My first attempt to build a birdhouse was a *dismal* failure; nails stuck out everywhere, and the paint collected in messy clumps.
syn: gloomy   *ant: cheerful*

MALEVOLENT   (mə lev´ ə lənt)   *adj.*   wishing harm toward; hostile
L. *malus* + *volere*, "to wish" = *wishing evil*
Erin says putting a "Kick Me" sign on Reggie's back was an innocent practical joke, but I think it was a *malevolent* gesture.
syn: spiteful   *ant: friendly*

MALICIOUS   (mə lish´ əs)   *adj.*   intended to hurt or harm
When Laurie forgot to give April an important phone message, April accused her of being *malicious*.
syn: damaging   *ant: helpful*

▥ In Latin, the adjective *animosus* meant "full of spirit" or "bold." As the noun form of this word passed into English, however, it came to mean not just boldness, but hostility.

▥ In the Middle Ages, certain days of the month were thought to be naturally unlucky. We no longer have these days in our calendar, but we do have a souvenir of the time: the word *dismal* can be traced to the medieval Latin phrase *dies mali*, meaning "evil days."

EXERCISES - UNIT TEN

Exercise I. Complete the sentence in a way that shows you understand the meaning of the italicized vocabulary word.

1. Rocky's *benevolent* nature was revealed when…

2. Because my parents were in *accord* when it came to the rules of the house, they never…

3. When I found out that the tumor was *benign*, I felt…

4. Many people felt *animosity* toward the television host because…

5. Our perfect picnic turned into a *dismal* one when we found out…

6. In response to the *discord* growing within the band, the guitarist tried to…

7. Although Sue thought Riley was *malevolent* toward her, I thought…

8. Because Jay has a *magnanimous* nature, he enjoys…

9. Although the mood at the party was generally *cordial*, when students from a rival school walked in, everyone felt…

10. In order to face your troubles with *equanimity*, you should…

11. I believe that the car wreck was not a *malicious* act on Roger's part, but instead,…

12. My uncle, who is my *benefactor*, has always…

Exercise II. Fill in the blank with the best word from the choices below. One word will not be used.

animosity	benefactor	cordial	malicious	*equanimity*

1. Although she felt some _____ toward the professor for giving her a bad grade, Linda did admire his intelligence.

2. As my official _____, Mr. Wells paid my college tuition.

3. Because Patty dreads fighting of any kind, she is glad her family reunions have all been _____ .

4. When Dory saw that Robert had fallen down, she smiled in _____ glee.

Fill in the blank with the best word from the choices below. One word will not be used.

benign   magnanimous   discord   benevolent   accord

5.   You could almost feel the _____ in the room grow when the opposing candidates took the stage together.

6.   Although Tina tries hard to be _____, she still feels selfish sometimes.

7.   The two friends got along well because they were in _____ about almost everything.

8.   What I thought was going to be a hard punch on my shoulder turned out to be only a(n) _____ tap.

Fill in the blank with the best word from the choices below. One word will not be used.

benevolent   equanimity   discord   malevolent   dismal

9.   Dropping a banana peel accidentally is one thing, but deliberately placing it where you know someone will be walking is a(n) _____ act.

10. After a pep talk from his older brother, Benji was able to face his fear of heights with _____.

11. The sky is rather gray and _____, but I'm still in a good mood.

12. The nurses in the hospital were some of the most _____ people I had ever met.

Exercise III. Choose the set of words that best completes the sentence.

1.   Because his actions were in _____ with his beliefs, Charles could endure any amount of questioning with calmness and _____.
     A.   discord; benevolence
     B.   benevolence; animosity
     C.   accord; equanimity
     D.   equanimity; accord

2.   Chris became a living example of the power of forgiveness when he answered a cruel, _____ act with a decent and _____ gesture.
     A.   magnanimous; benevolent
     B.   malevolent; malicious
     C.   benign; dismal
     D.   malicious; magnanimous

3.   Even if the visiting speaker is perfectly _____, she will likely be treated with _____ by the group that has
      gathered to protest her appearance.
      A.   cordial; animosity
      B.   benevolent; accord
      C.   malevolent; equanimity
      D.   malicious; accord

4.   The tension and _____ between my father and me lessened the chances that he would serve as my _____
      while I tried to write my novel.
      A.   accord; animosity
      B.   animosity; accord
      C.   discord; benefactor
      D.   discord; equanimity

5.   Since she was suspicious, Becky interpreted a _____ comment about her hair as unfriendly and _____.
      A.   benign; malicious
      B.   benign; cordial
      C.   dismal; malevolent
      D.   malevolent; magnanimous

Exercise IV. Complete the sentence by inferring information about the italicized word from its context.

1.   If Simone visits a friend's house and is greeted in a *cordial* manner, she will probably assume her
      friend feels…

2.   If the vet says the growth he found on your beloved pet is *benign*, you will probably feel…

3.   If customers react with *animosity* to a pitch by a door-to-door salesman, we can assume they want
      him to…

**Exercise V. Fill in each blank with the word from the Unit that best completes the sentence, using the root
      we supply as a clue. Then, answer the questions that follow the paragraphs.**

An immigrant. A philanthropist. A ruthless business-man. Andrew Carnegie was all of these and more. Born on November 25, 1835, into a working-class family in Scotland, Carnegie rose to be the second-richest man in the world and the father of his own steel empire.

Carnegie was the older of two children. His father was a skilled weaver, but the Industrial Revolution threatened his job and other manual labor jobs. As a result, when Carnegie was twelve, his family immigrated to the United States and settled in Pittsburgh. Though the move was a success, the _____ (MAL) living conditions were worse than in their old hometown. Andrew's father was unable to find steady work, but his mother got a job binding shoes.

Carnegie landed his first job in a textile mill, earning $1.20 a week. The young but already aggressive worker then became a steam engine tender and telegraph operator. By 1853, he was working for the Pennsylvania Railroad as a personal telegrapher and assistant earning $35 a month.

In 1859, Carnegie was named Railroad Superintendent at a salary of $1,200 a year. Carnegie soon formed the Keystone Bridge Company, which constructed railroad bridges out of iron, instead of wood. Seven years later, he left the Pennsylvania Railroad, expanded Keystone Bridge, and obtained contracts for constructing the Brooklyn Bridge, New York City's elevated railways, and other lucrative projects around the world. Around 1873, he formed the Carnegie Steel Company and began building skyscrapers and other structures. By controlling nearly all aspects of the steel industry, Carnegie Steel quickly became one of the largest American businesses ever.

But, while he was successful at turning a profit, he wasn't a success at employee relations. Carnegie pushed his workers to the breaking point by making them work twelve-hour days, seven days a week, with only one day off during the year.

Not surprisingly, a strike began in 1892. While on vacation in Scotland, Carnegie wired his partner to settle the _____ (CORD), but violence erupted, and ten people were killed. Carnegie later wrote in his autobiography that the incident was a low point in his life, but he never accepted any responsibility for the deaths.

Later in life, in numerous _____ (ANIM) gestures, Carnegie gave away much of his enormous wealth to build and benefit libraries, churches, schools, and colleges across the nation and around the world. In 1900, he sold his Pittsburgh steel empire for more than $400 million and retired. By the time of his death in 1919, the millionaire _____ (BENE) had given away $350 million, much of which still benefits people today.

1. What is the main idea of the passage?
    A. Carnegie had to immigrate to the United States.
    B. Libraries, schools, and churches benefit many people.
    C. Carnegie was a shrewd businessman and philanthropist.
    D. Union disputes often end in violence.

2. What factor brought Carnegie's family to the United States?
    A. famine
    B. disease
    C. civil war
    D. the Industrial Revolution

3. To which of the following did Carnegie donate his money?
    A. other businesses
    B. libraries, churches, schools
    C. orphanages
    D. hospitals

4. With which of these statements would Carnegie probably most agree?
    A. The union dispute was the low point of his life.
    B. His family's move to Pittsburgh was a mistake.
    C. Wealthy people should not share their money.
    D. Working as a telegraph assistant was a lucrative job.

Exercise VI. Drawing on your knowledge of roots and words in context, read the following selection and define the italicized words. If you cannot figure out the meaning of the words on your own, look them up in a dictionary. Note that *ficiary* means "the one making, doing," and *content* means "satisfied."

Although she was the *beneficiary* of several hours of individualized tutoring, Monica was *malcontent* over her performance on last week's algebra exam. Despite having received free help from her neighbor, she still got a poor grade. When her teacher returned her test with a grade of 60%, Monica was immediately filled with a sense of dissatisfaction and sorrow.

UNIT ELEVEN

JUR
Latin JURARE, "to swear, to vow"
Latin JUS, JURIS, "law"

PERJURY   (pûr´ jər ē)   *n.*   the breaking of a legal oath
L. *per*, "against" + *jurare* = *to swear against*
The store manager swore at the trial that he had no information about the robbery; when he was caught lying, police charged him with *perjury*.
syn: dishonesty   ant: fidelity

ABJURE   (ab jōōr´)   *v.*   to swear off; to renounce
L. *ab*, "off, away from" + *jurare* = *to swear off*
After his fellow club members turned against him in the meeting, Peter *abjured* all contact with them.
syn: renounce   ant: endorse

CONJURE   (kän´ jər)   *v.*   to bring forth, especially through words
L. *con*, "together" + *jurare* = *to swear together with magical aid*
In the opening of the book, the author *conjures* up an image of his boyhood farm.
syn: evoke

DOMIN
Latin DOMINOR, DOMINARI, "to rule; to dominate"

PREDOMINANT   (prē däm´ i nənt)   *adj.*   being most evident or apparent
L. *pre*, "before" + *dominari* = *ruling before all others*
Although there are flashes of color here and there in the painting, black is the *predominant* shade.
syn: leading   ant: unimportant

DOMINEERING   (däm ə nēr´ ing)   *adj.*   forcing others to obey
Lucy's little sister is so *domineering* that she often orders the whole family, including her parents, around.
syn: bossy   ant: submissive

INDOMITABLE   (in däm´ it ə bəl)
        adj.   unbeatable; resilient
L. *in*, "not" + *dominari* = *unable to be dominated*
Rebecca's *indomitable* courage helped her survive her illness.
syn: invincible   ant: weak

The snowman's strength was INDOMITABLE, but villagers thought he was ABOMINABLE.

Notes (left margin):

▦ *The Latin word* jus *refers to a system or body of law.*

▦ *I abjure cigarettes, but I have stopped smoking them at least twenty other times before.*
— Anonymous

▦ *In the United States, the government has the right of* eminent domain, *which allows it to take private property that is needed for public use.* Domain, *meaning "that which is ruled," is from* dominari.

CRAT, CRAC
Greek KRATEIN, "to rule"
Greek KRATOS, "power"

ARISTOCRACY   (ar ə stäk´ rə sē)   *n.*   a group of the most wealthy and privileged
G. *aristos*, "best" + *kratein* = *rule by the best*
Members of the country's tiny *aristocracy* had private beaches for swimming.

THEOCRACY   (thē äk´ rə sē)   *n.*   a government ruled by a religious leader
       or figure
G. *theos*, "god, holy" + *kratein* = *rule by religious authority*
The *theocracy* in the country ended when the high priests representing the gods
were caught stealing from the people.

BUREAUCRAT   (byōōr´ ə krat)   *n.*   a minor official
L. *bura*, "cloth that covers a desk" + *kratein* = *desk power*
The councilman nominated several unqualified candidates to city positions,
leading to an increase in the number of *bureaucrats* in the city's government.

LEG
Latin LEX, LEGIS, "law"

LEGITIMIZE   (lə jit´ ə mīz)   *v.*   to give credit or recognition to
The police officer feared that giving the criminals any media attention at all would
legitimize their group's existence.
syn: validate   *ant: undermine*

PRIVILEGED   (priv´ ə lijd)   *adj.*   available only to a special few; entitled to
       something special
L. *privus*, "one's own" + *legis* = *one's own law*
As a member of the most secret intelligence operations, Vergil was entitled to
privileged information.
syn: confidential   *ant: common*

LEGISLATIVE   (lej´ is lāt iv)   *adj.*   having to do with the law
L. *lex* + *latum*, "bear, carry" = *law-bearing*
In one particularly chaotic *legislative* session, a law was passed, repealed, and
passed again.

⚖ *An autocracy (autos, "self" + kratein) is a government ruled by one person with total power, a dictatorship.*

⚖ *The Latin word lex, as opposed to jus, means "an individual or particular law."*

⚖ *The government of the United States is a device for maintaining in perpetuity the rights of the people, with the ultimate extinction of all privileged classes.*
—Calvin Coolidge

EXERCISES - UNIT ELEVEN

Exercise I. Complete the sentence in a way that shows you understand the meaning of the italicized vocabulary word.

1. When Nick *abjured* the art movement he himself had founded, his fellow artists…

2. America is clearly not a *theocracy*, since…

3. In contrast to the more *domineering* players on the baseball team, Tommy was…

4. We knew one of the witnesses had committed *perjury* because…

5. In a system absolutely controlled by the *aristocracy*, money tends to…

6. The *legislative* powers of the government were called into question when…

7. Ted wanted to run for public office, but his wife feared he might become a *bureaucrat* because…

8. In order to *conjure* an image of an absolute peace, the author…

9. The *predominant* mood among the smiling children was one of…

10. The runner's *indomitable* energy brought him…

11. The two boys with backstage passes felt *privileged* because…

12. Scientists feared that the eclipse would *legitimize* people's superstitions because…

Exercise II. Fill in the blank with the best word from the choices below. One word will not be used.

perjury   theocracy   privileged   domineering   abjure

1. Citizens in the country's religious minority risked arrest and imprisonment by members of the governing _____.

2. At the sports banquet, Jack was given a(n) _____ seat at the head table with the coach.

3. The official warned me that I would be committing _____ if any part of my testimony turned out to be untrue.

4. Gretchen is a great boss because she is strong and decisive without being _____.

Fill in the blank with the best word from the choices below. One word will not be used.

abjure	aristocracy	legislative	legitimize	indomitable

5. Showing _____ courage, the dog swam into the river and saved his master from drowning.

6. Joan of Arc would not _____ her beliefs even under penalty of death by fire.

7. The poorer people of a country often cannot compete with the demands of the _____.

8. Television programs, in trying to be "cutting edge," often _____ violence instead of speaking out against it.

Fill in the blank with the best word from the choices below. One word will not be used.

conjure	legislative	abjure	predominant	bureaucrat

9. Whereas forests and pastures once covered Hancock County, now shopping malls and golf courses are _____.

10. The _____ body of the government balances the executive branch.

11. After the accident, Frank could not _____ up a single memory of the previous ten years.

12. Although he insisted on strict conformity with the rules, the county sheriff did not consider himself a(n) _____.

Exercise III. Choose the set of words that best completes the sentence.

1. Jeff's stories about his bossy sister _____ a picture of a woman so _____ that she gives orders to total strangers.
    A. abjure; domineering
    B. conjure; domineering
    C. legitimize; legislative
    D. abjure; predominant

2. Although the country was technically a(n) _____ run by leaders of one Church, the government worked hard to _____ and recognize other religions.
    A. theocracy; legitimize
    B. bureaucrat; conjure
    C. aristocracy; abjure
    D. perjury; legitimize

3.   Although some members of the party chose to _____ the president's beliefs, the _____ feeling was one
      of support.
      A. domineer; legitimize
      B. perjure; theocratic
      C. legitimize; indomitable
      D. abjure; predominant

4.   Pierre, who has never had much money, hates the _____ in his country so much that he would commit
      _____ to prove a point if he felt he had to.
      A. bureaucrats; theocracy
      B. privileged; aristocracy
      C. aristocracy; theocracy
      D. aristocracy; perjury

5.   Sheila had the _____ opportunity to accompany the _____ runner on the last leg of his tenth successful
      marathon.
      A. indomitable; predominant
      B. predominant; legislative
      C. domineering; privileged
      D. privileged; indomitable

Exercise IV. Complete the sentence by inferring information about the italicized word from its context.

1.   If Jessica complains that her swim coach is too *domineering*, she probably thinks the coach should…

2.   If the judge warns Ted not to commit *perjury*, he may be expecting Ted to…

3.   When DJ *abjures* his loyalty to his favorite basketball team, we can assume he feels…

**Exercise V. Fill in each blank with the word from the Unit that best completes the sentence, using the root
      we supply as a clue. Then, answer the questions that follow the paragraph.**

Franklin Delano Roosevelt (FDR) was the thirty-second president of the United States, holding office from 1933 until his death in 1945. Elected to the presidency four times, FDR served longer than any other president did.

Roosevelt was a member of the American _____ (CRAC), born into a family of wealth and social standing. He was a cousin of Theodore Roosevelt, who was president of the United States from 1901-1909. FDR was educated in a prestigious private school; he graduated from Harvard and attended Columbia Law School. Instead of practicing law, however, he entered politics in 1910 as a member of the Democratic Party. His _____ (LEG) background and eloquent speeches helped him gain wide attention and popularity.

Roosevelt's political career was interrupted in 1921, when he developed polio, a disease that left him dependent on crutches or a wheelchair. His _____ (DOMIN)

spirit, though, led him to return to politics, and after serving two terms as New York's governor, he ran for president.

Roosevelt defeated Herbert Hoover and became president in 1933, during the Great Depression. The economy was in shambles, and unemployment paralyzed the nation. He projected confidence, saying at his first inauguration, "The only thing we have to fear is fear itself." FDR proposed a "New Deal" for the country that introduced dramatic social changes, which, in turn, led to the development of broad _____ (LEG) support for governmental programs to overcome the Depression. Roosevelt used frequent radio messages, or "Fireside Chats," to inform and encourage the American public. He was the first president to understand the power of radio in gaining public support. Interestingly, he managed to have himself pictured in ways that minimized his use of crutches or a wheelchair, and most people did not realize the extent of his physical limitations.

As the country moved out of the Depression, FDR's priorities changed from economic restoration to national defense and international alliances. When the Japanese bombed Pearl Harbor in 1941, the United States entered World War II, and Roosevelt proved that he was an able wartime leader. Roosevelt did not live to see the Allied victory, however, because he died of a cerebral hemorrhage in 1945, just months before Germany surrendered in Europe and the Japanese admitted defeat in the Pacific.

1. Based on the passage, how do you know that FDR's family had a high "social standing"?
    A. His father believed Franklin could be president
    B. His cousin Teddy had already been president.
    C. In New York, he had a great deal of political influence.
    D. He attended and graduated from Harvard.

2. Polio was important in FDR's life because it
    A. forced him to wear leg braces.
    B. made him understand others better.
    C. was something he needed courage and persistence to overcome.
    D. made people vote for him because they felt sorry for him.

3. When Roosevelt became president, the country
    A. was in an economic depression.
    B. was a world leader.
    C. had overcome the Depression.
    D. had a strong army to fight in World War II.

Exercise VI. Drawing on your knowledge of roots and words in context, read the following selection and define the italicized words. If you cannot figure out the meaning of the words on your own, look them up in a dictionary. Note that *il*, from *in*, means "not," and *merit* means "worth, value."

The people of the small Kingdom of Perunia claimed that their current king was *illegitimate*. King Peldon had gained control of the country after murdering the heir to the throne and declaring himself ruler. This situation angered the Perunian people, as they favored a system of government that would promote people based on achievement. This *meritocracy* was realized as soon as King Peldon was overthrown.

UNIT TWELVE

RAP

Latin RAPERE, RAPTUM, "to snatch"
Latin RAPAX, "greedy; devouring"

RAPACIOUS (rə pā´ shəs) *adj.* seizing everything; greedy
A *rapacious* group of colonists seized all the land for themselves, leaving none for the people who arrived later.
syn: demanding   *ant: giving*

RAPT (rapt) *adj.* giving total attention to; captivated
As a program on birds played across the screen, the kittens sat *rapt* in front of the television.
syn: fascinated   *ant: inattentive*

SURREPTITIOUS (sûr əp tish´ əs) *adj.* hidden or secret; done without notice
L. *sub*, "beneath, secretly" + *raptum = snatched secretly*
With a *surreptitious* motion of his hand, the magician hid the coin in the scarf.
syn: stealthy   *ant: open*

CEP

Latin CAPERE, CAPTUM, "to seize, to take"

PERCEPTIBLE (pər sept´ ə bəl) *adj.* able to be noticed or felt
L. *per*, "through" + *captum = taken through (the senses)*
The wink that Kevin gave Laurel was so fast that it was barely *perceptible*.

SUSCEPTIBLE (sə sept´ ə bəl) *adj.* able to be influenced
L. *sub*, "beneath" + *captum = taken from beneath*
Ben felt that if he were too open minded, he would be *susceptible* to harmful ideas, so he lived in isolation.
syn: impressionable

PRECEPT (prē´ sept) *n.* an idea important to a system of beliefs
L. *pre*, "before, in advance" + *captum = taken before*
One of the main *precepts* of the religion is kindness to other living creatures.
syn: commandment

▥ Rapture, *from* raptum, *is a condition in which a person is seized by joy, so that he or she seems to be transported to a higher emotional plane.*

▥ *The* velociraptor *is a perfectly named dinosaur. The word comes from the Latin* veloc, *"rapid" +* rapere, *"to snatch," whereas* dinosaur *itself comes from the Greek* deinos, *"terrifying" +* sauros, *"lizard."*

VOR

Latin VORARE, VORATUM, "to eat"

VORACIOUS (vôr ā´ shəs) *adj.* devouring everything
The *voracious* locusts left a path of ruined crops a mile long.
syn: insatiable

The VORACIOUS eater needed a SPACIOUS refrigerator.

OMNIVOROUS (äm niv´ ər əs) *adj.* feeding on both animals and plants
L. *omnis*, "all, everything" + *vorare* = *eating everything*
My two brothers are strict vegetarians, but I consider myself *omnivorous*.

HERBIVOROUS (hər biv´ ər əs) *adj.* eating only plants
L. *herbis*, "grass, plants" + *vorare* = *eating grass*
Early American pioneers found lots of grazing land for their *herbivorous* animals.

CAD, CAS

Latin CADERE, CASUM, "to fall"

DECADENT (dek´ ə dənt) *adj.* overly luxurious and lacking moral discipline; excessive
L. *de*, "down from" + *cadere* = *falling down from (a noble or pure state)*
The billionaire's spoiled children wasted millions of dollars on *decadent* parties.
syn: wanton   *ant: restrained*

CADENCE (kā´ dns) *n.* a rhythmic rise and fall
The beautiful *cadence* of Jeff's voice as he read lulled us to sleep.

CASUALTY (kazh´ yəl tē) *n.* something or someone injured, killed, or eliminated
Grandmother complained that politeness was just one more *casualty* of a world that couldn't slow down.
syn: victim

▥ The organization "Meatless Mondays" came into existence during World War I with the government-sponsored slogan "Food Will Win the War." MM urges more people to become omnivores and eat more fruits and vegetables. According to them, simply cutting out meat one day a week will help to save the world's rainforests, which are being destroyed to raise beef. They feel that being a complete herbivore is too difficult for most people, but eating only meat, in other words being a strict carnivore, hurts the person, as well as the planet.

▥ In war, truth is the first casualty. — Aeschylus, 6th-century BCE Greek playwright

EXERCISES - UNIT TWELVE

Exercise I. Complete the sentence in a way that shows you understand the meaning of the italicized vocabulary word.

1.   Felix was a *casualty* of the last war, having...

2.   When the professor noticed one *rapt* listener in the midst of several bored-looking students, she...

3.   The hum of electricity was *perceptible* in the room because...

4.   The hawk showed its *voracious* appetite by...

5.   The slow and solemn quality of the poem's *cadence* had the effect of...

6.   Deer are completely *herbivorous* animals that eat...

7.   One of the main *precepts* of police forces all over the world is...

8.   Buying candy and cosmetics was considered *decadent* during the Great Depression because...

9.   The foreign army was *rapacious* in the tiny little village, and as a result,...

10. Rodney's exit from the building was *surreptitious* because...

11. Young Grace was *omnivorous*, but her friend Kate...

12. Harold is so *susceptible* to illness that...

Exercise II. Fill in the blank with the best word from the choices below. One word will not be used.

rapacious	rapt	surreptitious	casualty	perceptible

1.   The babies stared in _____ wonder at the fireworks spreading in the night sky.

2.   An eagle's _____ hunger will rarely be satisfied by one or two small field mice.

3.   With envy _____ to everyone in the room, Judy admired Olga's dress.

4.   Bo left the house in a _____ fashion, climbing out the window in the dark.

Fill in the blank with the best word from the choices below. One word will not be used.

casualty	decadent	herbivorous	precept	cadence

5.   Members were asked to observe the general _____ of the organization.

6.   My pet hamster is _____ so she gets plenty of lettuce and carrots to eat.

7.   Janet's horse is a _____ of the race, having broken its leg trying to jump a very high hurdle.

8.   Victor's experience in the luxurious hotels and restaurants of Las Vegas led him to believe it was a very _____ city.

Fill in the blank with the best word from the choices below. One word will not be used.

susceptible	rapacious	omnivorous	cadence	voracious

9.   Like a(n) _____ animal, the tornado consumed everything in its path.

10.   When my father decided to be a vegetarian, he had to renounce his _____ eating habits.

11.   Frank is _____ to every new idea that comes along, so he can't stick to anything.

12.   To write song lyrics, you must follow the _____ of the musical script.

Exercise III. Choose the set of words that best completes the sentence.

1.   Some _____ animals are _____ to diseases that can be contracted by eating meat or plants.
      A. herbivorous; rapacious
      B. rapt; herbivorous
      C. omnivorous; susceptible
      D. voracious; omnivorous

2.   Although his skating error was barely _____ to the judges, Sven knew it would make him a _____ of the fierce competition.
      A. herbivorous; precept
      B. perceptible; casualty
      C. rapacious; cadence
      D. rapt; casualty

3.   One of the fundamental _____ of marching band instruction is that the whole group must follow the drum major's _____.
      A. precepts; cadence
      B. casualties; precept
      C. cadences; precept
      D. cadences; casualty

4.   For a group of entirely _____ guests, the chef can prepare a meatless meal that is luxurious, even _____.
      A. surreptitious; perceptible
      B. rapacious; voracious
      C. decadent; herbivorous
      D. herbivorous; decadent

5.   If people weren't so _____ to flashy advertising, would we still look at enticing commercials with _____ attention?
      A. susceptible; rapacious
      B. susceptible; rapt
      C. rapt; rapacious
      D. rapacious; susceptible

Exercise IV. Complete the sentence by inferring information about the italicized word from its context.

1   If Patrice tells Cal, who is very *susceptible* to suggestion, to steal some candy, Cal may...

2.   If the sound that a kitten in a tree makes is not *perceptible* to a passerby, the passerby will probably...

3.   Once a *rapacious* coyote goes after a farmer's livestock, it will most likely...

Exercise V. Fill in each blank with the word from the Unit that best completes the sentence, using the root we supply as a clue. Then, answer the questions that follow the paragraphs.

Cross-country running, a sport that requires strength, endurance, and a(n) _____ (VOR) passion for excellence, is gaining popularity in high schools nationwide. Athletes participating in cross country do not merely run races. Taking special care to avoid injury, runners must negotiate a wide range of challenging terrains, constantly striving to shorten race times and improve stamina. Through training and discipline, cross-country runners always aim to make continued progress with each race, thus achieving significant personal victories with every competition.

A typical cross-country course measures approximately three miles in length. The terrain frequently consists of dusty flat ground, rocky slopes, steep hills, muddy embankments, and leaf-strewn forests. Since cross-country season spans early to late autumn, runners also encounter a variety of weather situations. They race during oppressive heat and through cold, numbing rain. They exert maximum effort and finish each course in a state of utter exhaustion. Because of these often-dangerous conditions, runners are particularly _____ (CEP) to ankle injuries and heat-related illnesses. However, with the right training and equipment, most cross-country runners can avoid these problems altogether.

A suitable cross-country training program consists of practice and proper nutrition. Running the actual courses regularly enables athletes to become familiar with the trails, developing a _____ (CAD) particular to each course. This, in turn, increases their speed and stamina, cutting seconds, or even minutes, off their times. When runners know the terrain, they also become less likely to be injured by obstacles on the course. Moreover, practice builds strength and resilience, which results in stronger athletes with fewer injuries.

The proper running shoes are essential equipment. Wearing the right shoes, ones designed specifically for distance running, helps reduce the risk of injury, as long as they fit correctly. Poorly fitted or improper shoes can result in unsure footing and may actually cause injuries.

Finally, the most important aspect of training is proper nutrition. Runners should eat a balanced diet in order to maintain healthy energy reserves. Without ample nutrients, they run the risk of injury from weakness and lack of proper nutrition. Furthermore, cross-country runners must also consume ample fluids to prevent dehydration, which can lead to overheating and injury.

Cross-country running requires a great deal of commitment and perseverance. Runners must train for years and take care of themselves with relentless dedication. Through practice and a strict program, these athletes constantly strive to improve their performance.

1. Which word best summarizes the most important quality of a cross-country runner?
    A. strength
    B. speed
    C. energy
    D. dedication

2. How long is a typical cross-country course?
    A. three kilometers
    B. three miles
    C. six miles
    D. two kilometers

3. Athletes avoid the risk of injury by
    A. practicing faithfully.
    B. taking frequent breaks from practice.
    C. practicing in dangerous conditions.
    D. practicing off the course.

4. The most important factor in being a healthy athlete is
    A. practice.
    B. equipment.
    C. nutrition.
    D. genetics.

Exercise VI. Drawing on your knowledge of roots and words in context, read the following selection and define the italicized words. If you cannot figure out the meaning of the words on your own, look them up in a dictionary. Note that _re_ means "back."

The medical students were presented with a _cadaver_ to work on during their recent laboratory session. Some of the students were a bit nervous about working on a dead body. The less squeamish students in the class, however, were quite _receptive_ to the challenge and quickly prepared themselves for the lesson.

UNIT THIRTEEN

FLU
Latin FLUERE, FLUCTUM, "to flow"

AFFLUENT   (a´ flōō ənt)   *adj.*   wealthy and privileged; well-to-do
L. *ad*, "toward" + *fluere* = *to flow toward*
In the more *affluent* neighborhoods of the city, it is not unusual for people to have several luxury cars.
syn: prosperous   *ant: impoverished*

SUPERFLUOUS   (sə pûr´ flōō əs)   adj.   additional to what is necessary; extra
L. *super*, "above" + *fluere* = *overflowing*
Ruben told me that the last paragraph in my article was *superfluous* because the other paragraphs already covered all the important information.
syn: nonessential, excessive   *ant: crucial*

MELLIFLUOUS   (mə li´ flōō əs)   *adj.*   sweetly flowing or sounding
L. *mel*, "honey" + *fluere* = *sweetly flowing*
The *mellifluous* notes of Meg's song reminded Jack of a gently running brook.
syn: harmonious   *ant: grating*

LEV
Latin LEVIS, "light"

LEAVEN   (lev´ ən)   *v.*   to make less heavy or serious
No matter how Angela tried to *leaven* the mood, everyone seemed determined to be miserable.
syn: lighten   *ant: dampen*

LEVITY   (lev´ ət ē)   *n.*   a lack of seriousness;
        a jolly or joking manner
The speaker's *levity* seemed out of place at the funeral.
syn: jollity   *ant: gloominess*

The Lecturer's Lack of LEVITY Left Leonard Lifeless.

ALLEVIATE   (ə lē´ vē āt)   *v.*   to make less painful or dangerous
L. *ad*, "toward" + *levis* = *to lighten toward*
Alice has developed a home remedy that will *alleviate* the symptoms of a bad cold.
syn: ease   *ant: aggravate*

> **III** *If you are* fluent *(from* fluere*) in a language, you can speak it flowingly, without stumbling over words.*

> **III** *To levy a tax is not, as you might expect, to lift or lighten it; rather, it is a way of raising money.*

LAPS

Latin LABI, LAPSUS, "to slip; to slide"

ELAPSE (ē laps´) *v.* to slip away; to go by
L. *e*, "out of" + *lapsus* = *to slip out of*
Many years had *elapsed*, and the farmer was eager to see his homeland again.

COLLAPSE (kə laps´) *n.* a complete failure and ruin
L. *con*, "together" + *lapsus* = *to slide together*
Some people fear the tax increase will bring about the *collapse* of the economy.

RELAPSE (rē´ laps) *n.* a falling back into an old illness or a bad habit
L. *re*, "back" + *lapsus* = *to slip back*
Since I decided to give up chocolate, I have not had a single *relapse*.
syn: setback

CED

Latin CEDERE, CESSUM, "to move along; to go"

RECEDE (rə sēd´) *v.* to move back or away from
L. *re*, "back" + *cedere* = *to go back*
As the ocean waves *receded*, the people on the shore saw a strange object lying on the sand.
syn: retreat   *ant: advance*

CONCESSION (kən sesh´ ən) *n.* something given up or yielded
L. *con*, "with" + *cessum* = *to move with*
Phil's parents have already made many *concessions* to their demanding son, so now, they are refusing to give him anything else.
syn: admission   *ant: refusal*

CEDE (sēd) *v.* to surrender
The two nations fought over the land for many years before one finally *ceded* it to the other.
syn: yield   *ant: withhold*

▥ *A relapse into the habit of smoking cigarettes, even after many years have elapsed, can cause a collapse of one's health.*

▥ *During the Civil War, the Southern states seceded from the United States; they formally moved apart from the Northern states. Secede is from se, "apart" + cedere.*

EXERCISES - UNIT THIRTEEN

Exercise I. Complete the sentence in a way that shows you understand the meaning of the italicized vocabulary word.

1. Natalie's voice was so *mellifluous* that people who called her store often…

2. In order to *leaven* the mood at the sad gathering, Ali…

3. The pain in my shoulder was *alleviated* by…

4. Although minutes seemed to *elapse* before the door opened, in reality,…

5. The *levity* in Sam's tone made it clear that he felt…

6. The complete *collapse* of the country's government was brought about by…

7. Nancy made a *concession* to Francis when she…

8. After the clouds *receded*, the weather…

9. Colin and Rebecca did not buy a house in the *affluent* section of town because…

10. When *superfluous* words are omitted from a piece of writing,…

11. Following his recovery, the ill patient had a brief *relapse* caused by…

12. My uncle would never *cede* the property to his neighbor because…

Exercise II. Fill in the blank with the best word from the choices below. One word will not be used.

relapse	leaven	cede	concession	affluent

1. One major _____ that Dan made to his mother was promising to come right home after school.

2. Fred gave up smoking two years ago, but had a(n) _____ and started again.

3. In order to be good sports, our team had to _____ the trophy to the other school.

4. The beautiful beach houses on the waterfront are owned by the most _____ people at the shore

Fill in the blank with the best word from the choices below. One word will not be used.

relapse   leaven   levity   recede   alleviate

5.   The minister frowned at the _____ in his congregation, and he warned the people to be more serious.

6.   A clown was brought in to _____ the atmosphere of the gloomy theater.

7.   My father's hairline has begun to _____, and nothing he can do will bring it forward again.

8.   To _____ his sister's burden, Will helped her with the yard work.

Fill in the blank with the best word from the choices below. One word will not be used.

mellifluous   superfluous   elapse   collapse   recede

9.   The file cabinet was stuffed with _____ papers that hadn't been needed in years.

10. In _____ tones, Melvin recited the poems he had written for English class.

11. Virginia's emotional _____ forced her to take a long vacation in the tropics.

12. Many years had _____ since the soldiers had seen one another.

Exercise III. Choose the set of words that best completes the sentence.

1.   After the uprising, the _____ upper class was forced to _____ both rights and property to the much larger group of poor and middle-class citizens.
     A.   mellifluous; alleviate
     B.   affluent; recede
     C.   superfluous; leaven
     D.   affluent; cede

2.   Although some of his jokes were off topic or _____, overall, Josh did a good job of _____ the mood.
     A.   mellifluous; elapsing
     B.   affluent; alleviating
     C.   superfluous; leavening
     D.   superfluous; ceding

3.   After a short time had _____, the soldier on guard saw the enemy troops _____ into the forest and disappear.
     A.   relapsed; collapse
     B.   relapsed; recede
     C.   alleviated; cede
     D.   elapsed; recede

4.   Because Reggie would make no _____ or alter his poor eating habits, he had a _____ and became ill again.
      A. relapse; concession
      B. concession; relapse
      C. collapse; concession
      D. levity; collapse

5.   Although the club owner joked about the singer at first, the _____ in his voice disappeared as he heard her _____ song.
      A. levity; mellifluous
      B. concession; affluent
      C. levity; affluent
      D. concession; superfluous

Exercise IV. Complete the sentence by inferring information about the italicized word from its context.

1.   If a man being chased by an angry mob suddenly sees the mob *recede*, he will likely feel…

2.   After the mayor eliminated all *superfluous* jobs in the city government, citizens…

3.   If a comedian wants to *leaven* the atmosphere in a club, he may start by…

Exercise V. Fill in each blank with the word from the Unit that best completes the sentence, using the root we supply as a clue. Then, answer the questions that follow the paragraphs.

The United States boasts the most productive economy in the world, and it depends on supply and demand. In this free-enterprise system, individual consumers (buyers) and private businesses (sellers) exercise most of the control. Buyers want the best value for their spending money, and sellers seek the most profitable price for their products. Moreover, American citizens are free to select their own employment, decide how to invest their earnings, and vote for government officials who decide economic policy. Despite this economic freedom, however, the United States has been unable to rid itself of the poverty that plagues many parts of the country.

Some financial experts believe that failure to reduce the poverty rate is due, in part, to the actual development of the labor market, in which citizens at the bottom lack the education and technical skills of people at the top. One group cannot afford to keep pace with technological advances and are, therefore, denied pay raises, health insurance, and other benefits. Meanwhile, those at the top have money to spend updating their skills, and they continue to get promoted. Since 1975, most of the actual increases in family income have gone to the most _____ (FLU) households. This seems to support the saying, "It takes money to make money."

This decrease of family income in the lower economic groups is reflected in the number of American families living below the poverty line. The poverty line, as defined by the federal government, is the minimum amount of income necessary to maintain a family of four. In 1990, that annual income level was $13,360. By 2015, it had grown to $24,250, despite changes in the Labor Department income guidelines. During the years that have _____ (LAPS) since 1990, the large number of people living at or below the poverty level has failed to _____ (CED).

Leveling the playing field for America's labor force of 140 million seems to be a long-term problem for the country said to have the most powerful economy in the world.

1.   What term best describes America's economic system?
     A.   three-tier labor market
     B.   free enterprise system
     C.   inflationary supply
     D.   socialist economic system

2.   In 1990, a family of four with an annual income of $13,360 was classified as
     A.   affluent.
     B.   rich.
     C.   unemployed.
     D.   impoverished.

3.   In this passage, what is meant by the statement "It takes money to make money"?
     A.   Original money is needed to make duplicate copies.
     B.   People need money to gamble.
     C.   Wealthy people can pay for education, which can then advance wealth.
     D.   Technology is the only means to extreme wealth.

4.   What statement best represents what the author is saying in this passage?
     A.   There are more poor Americans than there are rich Americans.
     B.   Poverty increases every year.
     C.   Poverty is a long-term problem for the United States.
     D.   Four people can live on $24,250 a year.

Exercise VI. Drawing on your knowledge of roots and words in context, read the following selection and define the italicized words. If you cannot figure out the meaning of the words on your own, look them up in a dictionary. Note that *pre* means "before," and *ex* means "out."

By choosing not to run for a third term, President George Washington set a *precedent* for all future holders of the office. This example lasted for over a hundred years, until Franklin Delano Roosevelt became the first and only president to *exceed* an eight-year term. Ironically, after the four-term, death-shortened presidency of FDR, Congress passed an amendment that restricted presidents to only two four-year terms in office. Congress cited Washington as a motivating reason behind the choice of eight years.

UNIT FOURTEEN

SEQUI, SEC
Latin SEQUI, SECUTUS, "to follow"

INCONSEQUENTIAL (in kän sə kwen´ shəl) *adj.* having no effect or
    importance
What once seemed like a major event in my life now seems entirely *inconsequential*.
syn: trivial   *ant: essential*

CONSECUTIVE (kən sek´ ū tiv) *adj.* following in order
L. *con*, "together with" + *secutus* = *following with*
For fourteen *consecutive* days, snow fell on the city.
syn: sequential

EXECUTION (ek sə kū´ shən) *n.* the way something is done
L. *ex*, "from" + *sequi* = *to follow from*
The spectators were astonished at the skater's perfect *execution* of a difficult jump.
syn: operation, performance

CUR, COUR
Latin CURRERE, CURSUM, "to run"

COURIER (kûr´ ē ər) *n.* one who carries and delivers
As a *courier*, Tom delivered packages to many interesting places.

INCUR (in kûr´) *v.* to bring about
L. *in*, "on, against" + *currere* = *to run against*
If you don't want to *incur* your math teacher's anger, you should finish your
homework.
syn: acquire   *ant: avoid*

RECURRENT (rē kûr´ ənt) *adj.* happening repeatedly
L. *re*, "again" + *currere* = *running again*
At the town meeting, some residents complained about the *recurrent* problem of
reckless driving.
syn: habitual   *ant: infrequent*

You probably know that a consequence (con, "with" + sequi) is a result. If something is of great consequence, it has significant results; it is meaningful. Something inconsequential has unimportant results and makes little difference.

There is no such word as reoccur; the correct word is recur (re, "again" + currere).

GRAD
Latin GRADI, GRESSUM, "to step"

GRADUALISM (gra´ jōō əl izm) *n.* a policy that involves taking slow, measured actions
When asked about how to deal with the nation's economy, the vice president recommended a kind of *gradualism*.

REGRESS (rē gres´) *v.* to go back to a less mature or less positive state
L. *re,* "back" + *gressum = to step back*
Whenever the two adult brothers got together, they seemed to *regress* to the age of thirteen.
syn: revert   *ant: improve*

DIGRESS (dī gres´) *v.* to move away from the topic at hand; to ramble
L. *dis,* "apart" + *gressum = to step apart; to step away*
The speaker started to *digress* from his intended subject, but he noticed the audience looking bored, so he stopped.
syn: depart   *ant: continue*

A hungry TIGRESS will not DIGRESS once she has spied her prey.

AMBL, AMBUL
Latin AMBULARE, AMBULATUM, "to walk"

AMBLE (am´ bəl) *v.* to walk casually; to stroll
Monique *ambled* up to the other children on the beach and asked what they were doing.
           ant: hurry

AMBULATORY (am´ bū lə tōōr ē) *adj.* able to walk
After months of physical therapy, the patient was *ambulatory* again.

PREAMBLE (prē´ am bəl) *n.* a passage or speech that introduces another longer passage or speech
L. *pre,* "before" + *ambulare = to walk before*
In the *preamble* to the US Declaration of Independence, Jefferson states the reasons the colonies are rebelling against Britain.

Gradualism is also a scientific theory that claims that evolution takes place through slow stages rather than sudden and violent changes.

The preamble to the Declaration of Independence begins, "We hold these truths to be self-evident…," but the preamble to the Constitution begins, "We the people of the United States…." They are certainly easy to get confused.

EXERCISES - UNIT FOURTEEN

Exercise I. Complete the sentence in a way that shows you understand the meaning of the italicized vocabulary word.

1. Tom's great-aunt was *ambulatory*, so she could…

2. Phil felt that he would make an ideal *courier* because…

3. A country may *regress* economically if its leaders…

4. Mrs. Moore did not want to *digress* in her lecture, so…

5. Matilda said the loss of the pennies was *inconsequential* because…

6. The pro skier *incurred* the scorn of the other skiers by…

7. Directly after the *preamble* to the speech was…

8. Because the battles along the border were *recurrent*…

9. The players' names were read in *consecutive* order so that…

10. The lone horse in the field would *amble* from one end to the other in order to…

11. Our company policy does not favor *gradualism*; instead, we plan to…

12. The skateboarder's *execution* of the difficult move was spoiled by…

Exercise II. Fill in the blank with the best word from the choices below. One word will not be used.

preamble   digress   recurrent   gradualism   courier

1. Writing a _____ to a speech is easy if you follow a general outline.

2. The Queen's _____ was so loyal that he risked his life to deliver her message.

3. If you have _____ hunger pangs, you should start eating a small snack between your main meals.

4. When the war began, the news anchor _____ from his written script to comment on the events of the day.

Fill in the blank with the best word from the choices below. One word will not be used.

ambulatory	recurrent	execution	regress	inconsequential

5.   Charles believes that the grades he gets in English are _____ because he is going to major in biology.

6.   No matter how many obedience classes the dog attended, she always seemed to _____ to her old patterns of behavior.

7.   After the accident, the teenager had to use crutches in order to be _____ at all.

8.   The _____ of the plan went off without a hitch.

Fill in the blank with the best word from the choices below. One word will not be used.

courier	amble	consecutive	incur	gradualism

9.   Let's _____ over to the park and relax on the bench.

10.   When the _____ recommended by his principal advisors failed to work, the chairman called for more drastic measures.

11.   The lawyer said that if we didn't have insurance, we would _____ a fine in addition to paying for the damages.

12.   When the tennis champ lost three _____ games, fans began to wonder if she had lost her touch.

Exercise III. Choose the set of words that best completes the sentence.

1.   Although most of the patients on the sixth floor regained their coordination and became _____ again, a few _____ to a bedridden state.
   A.   consecutive; regressed
   B.   recurrent; digressed
   C.   ambulatory; regressed
   D.   inconsequential; incurred

2.   The expenses we _____ from the flood were _____ compared to the emotional stress we suffered.
   A.   digressed; ambulatory
   B.   regressed; recurrent
   C.   incurred; consecutive
   D.   incurred; inconsequential

3.   The successful _____ of the mission depended heavily on the _____ chosen to deliver the plans to the general.
      A. execution; courier
      B. gradualism; execution
      C. preamble; digression
      D. execution; regression

4.   The _____ to the handbook took up six _____ pages.
      A. preamble; consecutive
      B. execution; inconsequential
      C. gradualism; recurrent
      D. preamble; ambulatory

5.   Professor Lee's speech on evolution seemed to _____ along nicely until he _____ and began discussing his personal beliefs.
      A. regress; ambled
      B. amble; digressed
      C. digress; regressed
      D. incur; digressed

Exercise IV. Complete the sentence by inferring information about the italicized word from its context.

1.   If Norman's breakup with his girlfriend is *inconsequential* to him, he will probably NOT…

2.   Sherry's *recurrent* problems with her car's engine caused her to…

3.   If a lawyer *digresses* while discussing a will, the people waiting to hear about their inheritance may…

Exercise V. Fill in each blank with the word from the Unit that best completes the sentence, using the root we supply as a clue. Then, answer the questions that follow the paragraphs.

Throughout history, governments have killed criminals who violate their laws, and the United States is no different. These government-approved deaths create strong feelings, drawing hundreds of supporters and opponents who provide a media circus for news reporters, cameras, and bright television lights. Those who approve, administer, and perform the killings call it "capital punishment." Opponents call it the "death penalty."

Proposals to eliminate capital punishment have _____ (CUR) the anger of millions of US citizens who believe killers should die like their victims. Some resent the fact that killers suffer a death less violent and cruel than their victims did. Over the years, changes in the method of death have softened the penalty imposed by juries, judges, and courts. As recently as the 1950s, electrocution was the most common method. Today, lethal injection is the primary choice for execution, although states also use electrocution, gas, hanging, or a firing squad.

Opponents believe the only acceptable course is the elimination of the death penalty, and they cheered when the Supreme Court declared capital punishment unconstitutional in June 1972. The *Furman v. Georgia* case struck down state death penalty laws nationwide, changing sentences for hundreds of convicted murderers to life imprisonment.

Then, in 1976, the court overturned its *Furman* ruling and revived capital punishment. This revival started a flood of executions by the federal government and the 38 states that had capital punishment laws. By mid-May, 2016, 1,436 convicted killers had been executed in the US; since 2002, all but three had been put to death by lethal injection. Texas has executed over 537 people, more than three times as many as any other state has.

Today, more than 2,900 prisoners are awaiting execution. Most of them have a background of physical and economic problems. They often have low IQs and are high-school dropouts. Many of them grew up with violence and

_____ (CUR) crime, and are social misfits. They know poverty and lack the financial resources to hire lawyers for a competent trial defense. Many also were under the influence of drugs or alcohol at the time of their crimes and can't remember what they did. Whatever caused the violent actions, those who favor the death penalty point out that a dead killer will never kill again, while opponents want the money spent for imprisonment of these killers—up to $100 per day for each prisoner—to be used on programs to correct many common social conditions. Although few innocent people have been executed, opponents argue that a mistake cannot be undone. They believe the death penalty is an ineffective, simplistic response to violent crime.

By 2016, the trend has been moving away from capital punishment; a total of 11 states had it in their laws at that time.

1.   The US Supreme Court, acting on *Furman v. Georgia,*
     A.   abolished capital punishment.
     B.   established capital punishment.
     C.   killed 537 prisoners.
     D.   sentenced more than 2,900 prisoners to death.

2.   What is the most common method of execution today?
     A.   electrocution
     B.   lethal injection
     C.   firing squad
     D.   gas

3.   What characteristic is NOT among those listed in the backgrounds of many convicted murderers?
     A.   poverty
     B.   low intelligence
     C.   not fitting in socially
     D.   single-parent homes

4.   How many states did not have capital punishment in 1976?
     A.   31
     B.   17
     C.   12
     D.   18

Exercise VI. Drawing on your knowledge of roots and words in context, read the following selection and define the italicized words. If you cannot figure out the meaning of the words on your own, look them up in a dictionary. Note that *con* means "together," and *ag*, from *ad*, means "toward."

The serial killer was sentenced to serve twelve *concurrent* life terms in federal prison. The court ordered him to serve all twelve sentences at the same time because of the nature of his crimes and because of the length of the penalty. When questioned about the case, Assistant District Attorney Martha Frankheld said, "Today, we put one of the most *aggressive* murderers in American history behind bars. Tomorrow, our streets will be a bit safer, but our jobs are not done." Frankheld was alluding to the boldness of the killer who had kept authorities on a massive manhunt for a suspect for nearly three years.

UNIT FIFTEEN

JUNCT
Latin JUNGERE, JUNCTUM, "to join; yoke"

ENJOIN (en joyn´) *v.* 1. to command; to urge
                          2. to forbid
1. Niqua *enjoined* her sister not to tell their parents about the car accident.
2. The District Attorney *enjoined* his client from speaking about the case.

INJUNCTION (in junk´ shən) *n.* an order that legally prevents something
The judge issued an *injunction* to stop the suspect from leaving the country.
syn: prohibition

REJOINDER (rē joynd´ ər) *n.* an answer; a reply
L. *re*, "back" + *jungere* = to join back
The writer of the letter to the newspaper issued a *rejoinder* to his critics.
syn: retort

PART
Latin PARS, PARTIS, "part"

IMPARTIAL (im pär´ shəl) *adj.* having no bias or favor
L. *in,* "not" + *partis* = not partial
Though Maggie claims to have *impartial* feelings about her two cats, she secretly likes Mittens best.
syn: neutral   *ant: prejudiced*

PARTISAN (pärt´ i zən) *adj.* believing and acting
          on the ideas of a political party or group
During a particularly close election, our town was split along *partisan* lines.
syn: factional

The *PARTISAN ARTISAN* carved elephants only for the Republican Party.

IMPART (im pärt´) *v.* to give away; to share
L. *in,* "in" + *partis* = to take part in; to share
Before I set out on my own, my mother *imparted* some helpful advice about life to me.
syn: convey, relay   *ant: conceal*

Sidebar:

▥ To enjoin *literally means* "to place a yoke upon" *(i.e., to command). There is also, however, a meaning of "forbid," and from this we get* injunction.

▥ A conjunction *is a grammatical device that links words or sentences; some English conjunctions are* and, as, but, *and* because.

▥ A partita *is a musical piece divided into several sections.*

CLUS, CLUD
Latin CLAUDERE, CLAUSUM, "to close"

INCLUSIVE   (in klōō´ siv)   *adj.*   containing all; not keeping any out
L. *in*, "in" + *clusum = to close in*
I am looking for a more *inclusive* atlas because my current one has only a few maps.
syn: all-embracing   *ant: limiting, exclusive*

INCONCLUSIVE   (in kən klōō´ siv)   *adj.*   providing no clear answer or solution
L. *in*, "not" + *con*, "together" + *clusum = not closed together*
The detectives were sure the DNA test would help them catch the thief, but the results proved *inconclusive*.
syn: uncertain   *ant: definite*

PRECLUDE   (prē klōōd´)   *v.*   to prevent from happening
L. *pre*, "before" + *cludere = to close before*
Frank's car crash on Wednesday *precluded* his getting to the party on Thursday.
syn: hinder   *ant: foster*

CIS
Latin CADERE, CAESUM, "to cut"

PRECISE   (pri sīs´)   *adj.*   accurate; definite
L. *pre*, "before" + *caesum = to cut off before*
Scientists have been trying to perfect their new satellite system in order to make sure that the information it records about the asteroid is *precise*.
syn: exact   *ant: indefinite*

INDECISIVE   (in dē sī´ siv)   *adj.*   unable to make choices
L. *in*, "not" + *de*, "down" + *caesum = not cut down*
Doris was so *indecisive* that it took her hours to grocery shop.
syn: doubtful, hesitant   *ant: sure*

INCISION   (in si´ zhən)   *n.*   a cut made into something
L. *in*, "into" + *caesum = to cut into*
A careful *incision* in the false back of the book revealed hidden money.
syn: slice, score

▥ *A cloister (from clausum) is a building closed off from the world for the purpose of prayer and reflection.*

▥ *A caesura is a pause in the middle of a speech, line of a song lyric, or poetic line. Juliet says, "Romeo, Romeo, wherefore art thou Romeo?" There are two caesuras: between the repeating of his name and after the second "Romeo." Spoken with the pauses, the line is intended to show her love and longing for him. They slow down the line.*

EXERCISES - UNIT FIFTEEN

Exercise I. Complete the sentence in a way that shows you understand the meaning of the italicized vocabulary word.

1.   The commander *enjoined* his troops from...

2.   An *incision* had to be made to...

3.   The decision by the judge hardly seemed *impartial* because...

4.   The attendees at the Democratic Convention showed their *partisan* support by...

5.   On the tour of the ancient ruins, the guide *imparted*...

6.   In order to be *inclusive*, the surveyors must...

7.   Luke tried to come up with a good *rejoinder* when...

8.   An *injunction* was issued to force the construction company to...

9.   Having my arm in a sling will *preclude*...

10.   Alleged facts to prove the thief's guilt were *inconclusive*, so the jury...

11.   The dress pattern had such *precise* instructions that...

12.   Keith was *indecisive* about hiring a star as a co-host on his talk show, so...

Exercise II. Fill in the blank with the best word from the choices below. One word will not be used.

enjoin   impart   indecisive   preclude   incision

1.   The tree surgeon was _____ about cutting down the hundred-year-old elm.

2.   Having to cook the Thanksgiving dinner will _____ my going to the football game.

3.   A(n) _____ was made into the cowhide to make a pocket in the leather coat.

4.   The landlord _____ the tenants to pay a deposit for any pets living with them.

Fill in the blank with the best word from the choices below. One word will not be used.

       injunction   incision   partisan   impart   inconclusive

5.   Peter tried to defend his candidate without showing too much _____ sentiment.

6.   The union was forced to operate under a(n) _____ imposed by the court.

7.   The aging philosopher chose to _____ his secrets for peace to his followers.

8.   The consumer group's investigation of the supposed miracle cleaner had _____ results.

Fill in the blank with the best word from the choices below. One word will not be used.

       precise   inclusive   impartial   incision   rejoinder

9.   The author of the editorial issued a(n) _____ to people who disagreed with him.

10.   Nina had to work hard to stay _____ in the classroom; otherwise, her students would think she was playing favorites.

11.   A(n) _____ study of the Middle Ages will cover politics, religion, and culture.

12.   We had no trouble installing the wall switch thanks to the _____ instructions we got from the hardware store manager.

Exercise III. Choose the set of words that best completes the sentence.

1.   If the measurements of oxygen used in the experiments are not _____, your results will likely be _____.
    A. partisan; inclusive
    B. impartial; precise
    C. impartial; inconclusive
    D. precise; inconclusive

2.   We were _____ about choosing a car because no one was able to _____ enough information about the feature we wanted.
    A. inconclusive; enjoin
    B. indecisive; impart
    C. impartial; enjoin
    D. indecisive; preclude

3.   The finality in Mrs. Chekovsky's voice _____ any further sarcastic _____.
    A. imparted; injunction
    B. precluded; incision
    C. imparted; incision
    D. precluded; rejoinder

4.   Mr. Donnelli never takes sides; he feels that his Scout troop will succeed only if he is _____, and the
      group is _____ to everyone.
      A. impartial; precise
      B. imprecise; inconclusive
      C. inconclusive; partisan
      D. impartial; inclusive

5.   The head surgeon _____ the young student to make a(n) _____ across the patient's abdomen.
      A. imparted; rejoinder
      B. imparted; incision
      C. enjoined; incision
      D. enjoined; injunction

Exercise IV. Complete the sentence by inferring information about the italicized word from its context.

1.   If the man in line at the crowded donut store is *indecisive* about what he wants, the other customers
      may…

2.   An announcement that the financial situation of the company has *precluded* the awarding of bonuses
      might make the employees…

3.   If a newsman warns that *partisan* politics are endangering the city council's future, he probably thinks the
      council should…

**Exercise V. Fill in each blank with the word from the Unit that best completes the sentence, using the root
      we supply as a clue. Then, answer the questions that follow the paragraphs.**

When the atomic bomb was dropped on Hiroshima, Japan, on August 6, 1945, it was the result of years of scientific study. The United States, coming out of the Great Depression, took little notice when Adolf Hitler came to power in 1933 as Germany's new leader. America then became the unsuspecting beneficiary of excellent scientists, who were forced to leave the Third Reich because of their Jewish origins. One who came to this country was Albert Einstein.

One of the greatest thinkers of the 20th century, Einstein had won the Nobel Prize for Physics in 1921. In 1939, shortly before World War II began, Einstein learned of two German chemists who had split a uranium atom. He wrote to President Franklin D. Roosevelt, indicating that this advance could help Germany build an atomic bomb and recommending that the United States start to develop its own weapon. His urgings resulted in the Manhattan Project.

The Project was headed by Brigadier General Leslie Groves in 1942, who had previously overseen construction of the Pentagon. Groves was in charge of all aspects of the Manhattan Project, including the production and planning for use of this special weapon. He also set up facilities at Oak Ridge, TN, and Los Alamos, NM. At the same time, J. Robert Oppenheimer was appointed Director of the Manhattan Project. He was a brilliant professor of physics, leading research in the uses of subatomic particles. Under his leadership, the finest minds in physics set to work in solving the issues involved in developing such a bomb. Oppenheimer managed several thousand people, and he was often asked to _____ (PART) his knowledge to solve some of the many problems that continually troubled the Project.

It is perhaps ironic that the Germans decided not to pursue atomic research. The work was _____ (CLUD) by their lack of resources, and they thought they could win the war without it. Even after Germany surrendered in 1945, however, work on the bomb continued in the United States. The first practical bomb was successfully tested in July 1945; soon afterward, two bombs (nicknamed "Fat Man" and "Little Boy") were delivered to the Mariana Islands in the Pacific.

On August 5, 1945, President Harry S. Truman, who was anything but _____ (CIS), gave verbal permission for their use in the continuing war with Japan. On August 6, 1945, Colonel Paul Tibbets piloted the B-29 "Enola Gay" carrying "Little Boy" on the trip to Hiroshima. The other bomb, "Fat Man," was dropped from a B-29 on Nagasaki, Japan, on August 9, 1945. The world has not been the same since.

1. What best explains the main idea of this passage?
    A. The atomic bomb works, but is destructive.
    B. The development of the atomic bomb was difficult.
    C. Germany won the race to develop the atomic bomb.
    D. The United States developed and used the first atomic bomb.

2. The United States decided to work on an atomic bomb on the recommendation of
    A. President Roosevelt.
    B. Albert Einstein.
    C. General Groves.
    D. J. Robert Oppenheimer.

3. Who directed the Manhattan Project effort?
    A. Albert Einstein
    B. General Groves
    C. J. Robert Oppenheimer
    D. President Truman

4. Who flew the "Enola Gay" on its historic mission?
    A. Colonel Tibbets
    B. General Groves
    C. The Germans
    D. J. Robert Oppenheimer

Exercise VI. Drawing on your knowledge of roots and words in context, read the following selection and define the italicized words. If you cannot figure out the meaning of the words on your own, look them up in a dictionary. Note that *ad* means "toward," and *se* means "apart."

The Pattersons have decided to construct a new building *adjoining* their home. The new portion will connect their existing detached garage to the house. Additionally, they are planting several trees in their backyard in an attempt to create a *secluded* little area for rest and relaxation. Ever since Mr. Patterson retired, the couple has been seeking a place where they can go to hide from the stress of the world around them.

UNIT SIXTEEN

META
From the Greek prefix META, "after; changed; beyond"

METABOLISM   (mə tab´ ə lizm)   *n.*   the process through which an organism changes food into energy
G. *meta* + *ballein*, "to throw" = *to change by throwing*
As Ellen's diet changed, her *metabolism* changed, too.

METAMORPHOSIS   (met ə môr´ fə sis)   *n.*   a change in form; a transformation
G. *meta* + *morphe*, "shape" = *changed shape*
After several weeks, the tadpole's *metamorphosis* into a frog was complete.
syn: conversion, alteration

METAPHORICAL   (met ə fôr´ i kəl)   *adj.*   symbolic rather than literal
G. *meta* + *pherein*, "to carry" = *to carry beyond*
Mr. DeMarco had a hard time explaining to his class that they were not going on a real field trip, but a *metaphorical* one.
syn: figurative   *ant: actual*

AL
Latin ALIUS, "other, another"

INALIENABLE   (in âl´ ē ən ə bəl)   *adj.*   not able to be taken away
L. *in*, "not" + *alien* + *able*, "able to be" = *not able to be made other*
Although Michelle seems to think it's her *inalienable* right to interrupt people, few friends agree with her.

ALIENATE   (âl´ ē ən āt)   *v.*   to make hostile
Alison *alienated* her party guests by forcing them to listen to music they didn't like.
syn: offend   *ant: attract*

ALIAS   (âl´ ē əs)   *n.*   a name that is not one's true name
Following his testimony in a high-profile murder case, Jason Ryan assumed the *alias* "Steven Berger."

Metabolic originally meant "having to do with change"; in the late 19ᵗʰ century, it came to refer to the processes of living beings.

The word metamorphosis has a place in two major works of Western literature. The poet Ovid (43 BC-17 AD) called his collection of poems dealing with transformation the Metamorphoses; in The Metamorphosis, by Franz Kafka (1883-1924), the main character is transformed into a bug.

An alien can be a visitor from another planet or a person living in a country to which he or she is not native.

ALTER
Latin ALTER, "other"

ALTERATION (ôl tər ā´ shən) *n.* a change or modification
Any *alteration* in the plans at this point will force us to design an entirely new schedule.

ALTERNATE (ôl´ tər nāt) *v.* to go back and forth; to change from one thing to another
Teresa *alternates* between the two grocery stores because both have products she wants.

ALTERCATION (ôl tər kā´ shən) *n.* a fight or dispute
An *altercation* outside the nightclub led to the arrests of several customers.

SIMUL
Latin SIMULARE, SIMULATUM, "to imitate; to pretend; to appear to be"

SIMULATE (sim´ yōō lāt) *v.* to mimic; to imitate
The ride at the amusement park claims to *simulate* the experience of zero gravity.
syn: represent

DISSEMBLE (di sem´ bəl) *v.* to conceal the truth; to deceive
L. *dis*, "not" + *simulare* = to appear to be what one is not
Rather than *dissembling* when asked if he took the money, Clayton confessed to everything.
syn: deceive, counterfeit   *ant: reveal*

SEMBLANCE (sem´ bləns) *n.* a rough likeness
My mother demanded that I get my room into some *semblance* of order before our relatives came to visit.
syn: copy

While the police sketch was only a SEMBLANCE of a RESEMBLANCE, it was enough to catch the bad guy.

▥ An alter ego (*literally meaning "other self") is a personality adopted in addition to an original identity. There is another term that means almost the same thing as alter ego—alias. A person uses an alias in order to conceal his or her identity.*

▥ *The world in which we live is only a semblance of what it could—and should—be.*
—Anonymous

EXERCISES - UNIT SIXTEEN

Exercise I. Complete the sentence in a way that shows you understand the meaning of the italicized vocabulary word.

1.   Although she was frustrated at losing the contest, Agnes tried to *dissemble* by...

2.   Dad tried to avert an *altercation* between my sister and me by...

3.   The two bandits had to have *aliases* so they could...

4.   The author chose to describe her heroine using *metaphorical* language, rather than...

5.   The divorce of my friend's parents *alienated* them from their relatives, who...

6.   The builder had to *alternate* between adding wiring and connecting the plumbing because...

7.   My friend had to *simulate* a famous work of art in class, so he...

8.   Johanna couldn't believe the *metamorphosis* she saw in the plant after...

9.   Trying to achieve some *semblance* of beauty, Daphne...

10.   Peggy made the *alteration* to her dress by...

11.   After the stolen car was recovered, police gave *inalienable* ownership to Ed, because...

12.   When Denise decided to continue her fast, her *metabolism* began...

Exercise II. Fill in the blank with the best word from the choices below. One word will not be used.

semblance   altercation   simulate   inalienable   metabolism

1.   One _____ right given in the US Constitution is freedom of speech.

2.   We didn't really have a(n) _____; we just disagreed.

3.   Nothing in the creature's _____ allows it to produce energy quickly.

4.   To maintain any _____ of fairness, the members of a government must carefully govern themselves.

Fill in the blank with the best word from the choices below. One word will not be used.

dissemble	alteration	alias	simulate	metamorphosis

5. Any _____ to the building plan must be made before the final blueprint is provided.

6. There was no way Joan could continue to _____ her true identity, since everyone now knew who she was.

7. Once Cindy had successfully handled a crisis without anyone's help, her _____ from child to adult was complete.

8. Because the children had _____ escaping from a fire in a drill, they knew what to do when a real fire occurred.

Fill in the blank with the best word from the choices below. One word will not be used.

alienate	metamorphosis	alternate	metaphorical	alias

9. Don't _____ me from the study group just because I know the lessons better than any of you do.

10. The problem with speaking in _____ terms is that people might mistake what you say for the truth.

11. The numerous _____ the forger used made it difficult for police to catch him.

12. Does the paperboy _____ routes, or does he go in the same direction every morning?

Exercise III. Choose the set of words that best completes the sentence.

1. A heated _____ between the two party officials started because both felt _____ from the party.
   A. alteration; dissembled
   B. metamorphosis; alienated
   C. altercation; alienated
   D. semblance; alternated

2. Doctors tried to regulate the sick man's _____ so that he regained some _____ of a functioning digestive system.
   A. alias; semblance
   B. metabolism; alias
   C. metamorphosis; semblance
   D. metabolism; semblance

3.   In attempting to _____ the problem he had had with the machines at work, Sam made a major _____ to his own computer.
     A.   dissemble; altercation
     B.   simulate; alteration
     C.   alienate; metabolism
     D.   alternate; semblance

4.   Although the werewolf tried to hide his nightly _____ from the world, there came a time when he could _____ no longer.
     A.   alteration; alienate
     B.   metamorphosis; dissemble
     C.   metamorphosis; simulate
     D.   metabolism; simulate

5.   The check swindler _____ between different _____ so that he doesn't stay under any one name too long.
     A.   alienates; metamorphoses
     B.   simulates; semblances
     C.   dissembles; metabolisms
     D.   alternates; aliases

Exercise IV. Complete the sentence by inferring information about the italicized word from its context.

1.   If you hear that two baseball players were involved in an *altercation*, you will probably assume that the umpire…

2.   If Angie's friends *alienate* her at lunch, you will probably see her looking…

3.   If the child *dissembles* when asked about the missing cake, it is probably because she…

Exercise V. Fill in each blank with the word from the Unit that best completes the sentence, using the root we supply as a clue. Then, answer the questions that follow the paragraphs.

The American Revolutionary War was not meant to be a social revolution. It was a movement for independence and home rule started by a privileged minority. Nonetheless, the Revolution profoundly changed American society.

During the Colonial period, most political offices were held by wealthy men. Some of these men were involved in the earliest _____ (ALTER) with the British and became the leaders of the movement for independence. These patriots weren't interested in social change; they simply wanted the colonies to rule themselves and be independent from England. The new government that the patriots envisioned did not attempt to change the distribution of wealth or end discrimination based on class, race, or gender. In fact, most of the benefits of the American Revolution went to people like themselves: white male property owners.

As early as 1770, however, some farmers and craftsmen had begun to protest against the wealthy, powerful men who controlled local politics. After the war, these artisans and farmers organized and elected state representatives from their own ranks, giving them political power they never had before.

Women didn't fare as well, though. Although patriotic women assumed new responsibilities during the Revolutionary War, such as producing more cloth for soldiers' clothes and managing homes and farms in the absence of their husbands, the reforms promised by the Revolution did not extend to them. Some women lobbied for the right to own property and the right to vote, but they were unsuccessful.

Although workers, women, and the poor continued to feel _____ (AL) from political life, colonial society underwent a _____ (META) during the Revolutionary War. For one thing, the long war was costly and created soaring inflation. As goods grew more expensive, every family had to become more skilled at managing money and more concerned with its own welfare. The dollar was worth less and less, and farmers refused to sell their crops to the Continental Army for currency that was nearly worthless. Many farmers became politically active. Women led mobs that raided stores that sold overpriced bread, sugar, and tea. Some people were forced into subsistence farming. The social and economic structure underwent a further _____ (ALTER) when thousands of wealthy, conservative people who were loyal to Britain left the colonies. After years, the new emphasis on personal freedom led to the end of slavery in the North.

While the privileged minority who led and controlled the American quest for independence may not have intended a social revolution, they created one anyway. Life in the American colonies was fundamentally changed when a rigid class structure and the rule of a monarchy were replaced with individual liberty and representative government. This legacy of freedom and fairness was truly revolutionary.

1. What is the main idea of this essay?
    A. The American Revolution brought about profound social changes.
    B. The Revolutionary War was fought by farmers and craftsmen.
    C. Women did not fare well during the Revolutionary War.
    D. The war against Britain directly led to the end of slavery.

2. The original patriots wanted to
    A. stop discrimination.
    B. force people loyal to Britain to leave the colonies.
    C. rule themselves.
    D. improve the economy in the colonies.

3. The leaders of the movement for independence were
    A. artisans and farmers.
    B. British loyalists.
    C. white male property owners.
    D. elected officials.

4. What does the author think is the most important legacy of the American Revolution?
    A. Slavery was abolished in the North.
    B. Farmers became politically active.
    C. Women learned to manage households and farms.
    D. Class structure was replaced with individual freedom.

Exercise VI. Drawing on your knowledge of roots and words in context, read the following selection and define the italicized words. If you cannot figure out the meaning of the words on your own, look them up in a dictionary. Note that *en*, from *in*, is an intensifier.

Chicago is a musical about murder, revenge, the media, love, and fame. The tales of the *ensemble* are woven together with songs, dances, and some quick-paced dialogue. The show takes the lives of many characters to form a single, epic story. One of the highlights occurs in the second act, when Roxie Hart recounts her *alibi* to a jury. The audience knows that Roxie's story about where she was during the murder was completely crafted by her lawyer, Billy Flynn.

UNIT SEVENTEEN

MORT
Latin MORS, MORTIS, "death"

IMMORTALIZE   (i môr´ tə līz)   v.   to preserve in memory forever
L. *in*, "not" + *mortis* + *ize*, "to cause" = *to cause to live forever*
The courageous stand taken by the prime minister on that day *immortalized* him in the eyes of his people.
syn: memorialize   *ant: forget*

MORBID   (môr´ bid)   *adj.*   taking an unhealthy interest in unpleasant things
Susan had a *morbid* imagination, and she drew several hundred pictures of cemeteries.
syn: unwholesome

MORTIFY   (môr´ tə fī)   v.   to cause extreme embarrassment to
A scolding from his mother in front of his friends *mortified* Charles, and he ran out of the room.
syn: humiliate   *ant: delight*

MORIBUND   (môr´ i bund)   *adj.*   in a dying or deathlike state
Bonnie hoped the *moribund* old car would make it up one last hill so she could finally get home.
syn: deteriorating   *ant: reviving*

NEC, NOX, NIC
Latin NOCERE, NOXUM, "to hurt; to kill"
Latin NEC, NEXIS, "death"

NOXIOUS   (näk´ shəs)   *adj.*   harmful to physical or moral health
The *noxious* fumes of toxic chemicals filled the abandoned warehouse.
syn: foul   *ant: pleasant*

PERNICIOUS   (pər nish´ əs)   *adj.*   causing damage; harmful
L. *per*, "through and through" + *necis* = *thoroughly destructive*
Tina found that too much fertilizer was *pernicious* to her tomato plants.
syn: destructive   *ant: favorable*

▥ Rigor mortis (*literally, "stiffness of death"*) is the automatic stiffening of muscles that occurs after someone or something dies.

▥ *The Greek* nekros *also means "death" and appears in words like* necrosis.

BIO
Greek BIOS, "life"

BIODEGRADABLE (bī ō di grā´ də bəl) *adj.* able to be broken down naturally
G. *bios* + L. *de*, "down" + L. *gradus*, "going" = *going down by means of living things*
In order to help save the environment, many fast-food companies are finally using *biodegradable* packaging material.

SYMBIOTIC (sim bē ot´ ik) *adj.* mutually beneficial; supporting one another's
   life
G. *syn*, "together" + *bios* = *life together*
Although researchers once believed the two animals had a *symbiotic* relationship, a few scientists now think that one creature is simply scavenging off the other.

ANTIBIOTIC (an tī bī ot´ ik) *adj.* causing the death of living organisms,
   especially harmful ones
G. *anti*, "against" + *bios* = *against life*
The medicine's strong *antibiotic* properties make it useful for fighting bacterial infections.

VIV
Latin VIVERE, VICTUM, "to live"

VIVACIOUS (vi vā´ shəs) *adj.* cheerful and full
   of life
Donna is a *vivacious*, fun-loving girl who enjoys going out with her friends.
syn: merry, exuberant   ant: lifeless

VIVACIOUS VIVIAN and Sprightly Sue competed to win the prize for "Most Lively."

VIVID (vi´ vid) *adj.* making a strong impression on the senses; clear and sharp
The dream was so *vivid* that I still can't believe it wasn't real.
syn: striking   ant: faint

REVIVAL (rē vī´ vəl) *n.* the act or process of bringing back to life
L. *re*, "back" + *vivere* = *back to life*
The *revival* of a play that had not been produced for decades required much study on the part of the director and cast.
syn: reawakening   ant: expiration

There are at least three classifications of animals that live together. The first is parasitic, in which one animal feeds off another and harms it. A tapeworm is an example of parasitism. The second is symbiotic, in which both animals benefit. Clownfish live, unharmed, among the stinging tentacles of anemones, which get food in return for protection. The last category is commensal, in which one animal benefits, but does not harm or help the other. Hermit crabs use the shells of dead creatures for protection.

Vivisection (literally, "cutting up the living") is the practice of dissecting something while it is still alive to examine its organs or physical processes.

EXERCISES – UNIT SEVENTEEN

Exercise I. Complete the sentence in a way that shows you understand the meaning of the italicized vocabulary word.

1. Mom provided us with such a *vivid* picture of her wedding that…

2. Emma tried to *mortify* her easily shocked neighbors by…

3. The plant was found to have excellent *antibiotic* properties when…

4. The smell in the chemistry lab was so *noxious* that…

5. Some rumors are more *pernicious* than others because…

6. You should buy products that come in *biodegradable* packaging to…

7. The subject matter chosen by the poet was considered *morbid* because…

8. The *symbiotic* partnership between the big fish and the small one was clearly demonstrated when…

9. The *moribund* atmosphere of the hospital made Arlo feel…

10. Dolly was a *vivacious* girl, who often…

11. Famous athletes are often *immortalized* by…

12. We brought about the *revival* of the obscure novel by…

Exercise II. Fill in the blank with the best word from the choices below. One word will not be used.

vivacious	revival	morbid	pernicious	mortify

1. Tim's _____ interest in death and disease made him a great horror story writer.

2. Young people often respond to culture with a _____ of some of the fads of the previous generation.

3. Helen is afraid she will _____ her son if she hugs him in front of his classmates.

4. Some of the bad loans the major banks made turned out to be _____ to their state's economy.

Fill in the blank with the best word from the choices below. One word will not be used.

noxious   immortalize   vivid   antibiotic   vivacious

5.   The discovery of the mold's _____ properties was a huge benefit to the world of medicine.

6.   The freshly painted apartment was filled with a(n) _____ chemical smell.

7.   Unfortunately, the talk-show host was _____ forever by the embarrassing picture.

8.   Despite the common stereotype of nuns as dull and dreary, the Sisters at St. Clare's were cheerful and _____.

Fill in the blank with the best word from the choices below. One word will not be used.

moribund   vivid   morbid   symbiotic   biodegradable

9.   A sudden increase in wealth transformed the town from depressing and _____ to exciting and full of life.

10.   In an ideal ecosystem, all organisms would be in _____ relationships with one another.

11.   A _____ imagination is an excellent asset for a writer.

12.   Substances that are not _____ stay in landfills for years without decomposing.

Exercise III. Choose the set of words that best completes the sentence.

1.   Maggie's grandmother still has _____ memories of the day Neil Armstrong was _____ for being the first American on the moon.
      A.   vivid; mortified
      B.   pernicious; mortified
      C.   moribund; vivacious
      D.   vivid; immortalized

2.   When unsanitary conditions brought about a(n) _____ of the disease, Anthony had to take another dose of _____ pills.
      A.   symbiosis; antibiotic
      B.   revival; antibiotic
      C.   revival; symbiotic
      D.   antibiotic; noxious

3.   Elle, a _____, fun-loving girl, has been involved in some stunts that would _____ her mother.
      A.   morbid; immortalize
      B.   vivacious; immortalize
      C.   symbiotic; mortify
      D.   vivacious; mortify

4.   While indulging in _____ or tragic thoughts was once thought to be a harmless habit, "
      psychologists now warn that it can be _____ to one's overall mental health.
      A.   morbid; pernicious
      B.   moribund; noxious
      C.   pernicious; moribund
      D.   biodegradable; vivacious

5.   _____ chemical fumes from the new factory soon made the surrounding neighborhood a deserted, _____
      area.
      A.   Noxious; biodegradable
      B.   Noxious; moribund
      C.   Vivacious; vivid
      D.   Antibiotic; vivacious

Exercise IV. Complete the sentence by inferring information about the italicized word from its context.

1.   If a critic describes an art form as *moribund*, the critic probably does NOT feel that…

2.   If Celine was *mortified* by an experience at school, she probably wanted to…

3.   If a nutritionist points out the many *pernicious* features of a particular diet, he probably thinks the people
      on the diet should…

**Exercise V. Fill in each blank with the word from the Unit that best completes the sentence, using the root
      we supply as a clue. Then, answer the questions that follow the paragraphs.**

Chances are that you owe your life to a medicine that _____ (MORT) the name of Sir Alexander Fleming. That medicine, penicillin, may have saved the lives of your parents or grandparents. Penicillin's ability to cure people of many once-fatal bacterial infections has saved so many lives that one can readily understand why it was once called a miracle drug. Today, you would be shocked to hear of someone dying from an infection that started in a scratch, but, even in the 1930s, many people were dying from such infections.

Penicillin originates from a specific group of molds. The drug is a(n) _____ (BIO) and functions by preventing bacteria from forming new cell walls. One by one, the bacteria die because they cannot complete the process of cell division that produces two bacteria from a single parent.

Sir Alexander Fleming, a British doctor and bacteriologist, discovered penicillin in 1928 during his development of lysozyme, a substance that kills bacteria that are not _____ (NIC). He noticed that a blue mold had accumulated in one of his samples, which he had left on a table. He concluded that the blue mold could be some kind of medicine because it had dissolved the bacteria around its outer edge. What the doctor observed were the effects of penicillin, but he was unable to isolate the drug itself. At the same time that a group of British scientists were making progress on Fleming's work, World War II was beginning in Europe, and when the Germans began bombing London in 1941, the main research and production of penicillin was moved to the United States. Work began on how to efficiently make penicillin in large enough quantities to treat thousands of soldiers. As destruction from the war grew, so did interest in penicillin. Scientists knew that they were in a race against death because infections were as likely to kill wounded soldiers as their wounds were.

1.   Penicillin
      A. can kill all types of bacteria.
      B. was discovered in the 19th century.
      C. is a type of bacteria.
      D. is a type of mold.

2.   Which statement best describes the author's method of relaying information in the passage?
      A. fact follows fact
      B. conclusion follows analysis
      C. past follows present
      D. result follows inference

3.   Which statement is true of Dr. Fleming?
      A. He was part of a team that isolated penicillin.
      B. He was part of the team that discovered penicillin.
      C. He researched substances that kill bacteria.
      D. He discovered penicillin in 1938.

Exercise VI. Drawing on your knowledge of roots and words in context, read the following selection and define the italicized words. If you cannot figure out the meaning of the words on your own, look them up in a dictionary. Note that *polis* means "city."

In the Roman Empire, people were buried in *necropolises* outside of the city walls. These areas, much like today's cemeteries, allowed family members and friends the opportunity to have a place to visit deceased loved ones. Necropolises were first constructed when the Emperor saw a *viable* solution to removing the numerous disease-ridden corpses from within the walls of major cities. The idea worked, and the creation of these Roman cemeteries helped to lessen the spread of many illnesses.

UNIT EIGHTEEN

COGN
Latin COGNOSCERE, COGNITUM, "to know"

INCOGNITO (in käg nē´ tō) *adj.* disguised as someone other than oneself
L. *in*, "not" + *cognitum* = *not known*
Having been mobbed by admirers one too many times, the actor now goes *incognito* when he has to appear in public.
syn: masked   *ant: known*

COGNITIVE (käg´ ni tiv) *adj.* relating to the processes of thought
Learning to distinguish shapes and colors is part of a baby's *cognitive* development.

COGNIZANT (käg´ ni zənt) *adj.* aware
When Tasha became cognizant of a problem with the rocket, she notified the engineers.
syn: conscious   *ant: unaware*

The COG isn't COGNIZANT of its role in the machine.

SOPH
Greek SOPHOS, "wise"

SOPHISTICATE (sə fis´ ti kət) *n.* one well traveled and knowledgeable about culture, etiquette, and/or fashion
Since I am unable to distinguish a salad fork from an ordinary fork, I hardly consider myself a *sophisticate*.

SOPHISTRY (säf´ is trē) *n.* the use of trickery or false logic in arguments
At first, Brenda was convinced by the argument, but she later decided it was nothing but *sophistry*.
syn: deception   *ant: honesty*

SOPHOMORIC (säf môr´ ik) *adj.* not highly developed; crude
G. *sophos* + *moros*, "fool" = *wise fool*
I found Greg's sense of humor *sophomoric*, but he was funny nonetheless.
syn: foolish, immature   *ant: mature*

▥ Cognitive *skills include calculating, analyzing, examining, predicting, or any others that require the use of reason.*

▥ A sophomore, *as you may know, is someone at an intermediate level in school. While it is certainly not true that all* sophomores *are "wise fools," they are stuck with the name until they can move up a grade.*

NOMEN
Latin NOMEN, NOMINIS, "name"

NOMINAL (näm´ ə nəl) *adj.* in name only; not completely true
The *nominal* purpose of the club was to discuss ancient coins, but the members usually argued about politics.
syn: supposed   *ant: real*

DENOMINATION (dē näm ə nā´ shən) *n.* a subcategory or subgroup
L. *de*, "from" + *nominatum = named from*
Within their groups, the children broke into smaller *denominations* based on their backgrounds, interests, and personalities.

NOMENCLATURE (nō´ min klā tchər) *n.* an official system of naming
L. *nomen* + *calator*, "caller" = *called by name*
The ancient system of *nomenclature* was so complicated that no one could remember the official name of anything.

ONYM
Greek ONOMA, "name"

SYNONYMOUS (si nän´ ə məs) *adj.* meaning the same as
G. *syn*, "together with" + *onoma = with the name*
The pirate's name became *synonymous* with crime and violence.
syn: interchangeable   *ant: different*

ANONYMOUS (ə nän´ ə məs) *adj.* not revealing one's identity
G. *a*, "not" + *onoma = no name*
An *anonymous* donor gave several million dollars to the homeless shelter.
syn: unnamed   *ant: known*

ANTONYM (an´ tə nim) *n.* a word that means the opposite of another word
G. *anti*, "against, opposite" + *onoma = opposite name*
Instead of using the right word in my essay, I accidently used its *antonym*.

▥ *A nom de plume (from the French for "name of the pen" or "pen name") is a name taken by an author who wishes to conceal his or her identity: a nom de guerre (from French for "name of war; war name," dating to the time when French army officers took special military names) is simply an assumed name or alias.*

▥ *The word denomination often refers to a particular religious group.*

EXERCISES - UNIT EIGHTEEN

Exercise I. Complete the sentence in a way that shows you understand the meaning of the italicized vocabulary word.

1. It is often useful to know the *antonym* of a word because…

2. From the *nomenclature* of a group of minerals, we can tell…

3. Many religious *denominations* are contained in…

4. Famous people often travel *incognito* so that…

5. Asked about her favorite places to dine, the young *sophisticate* answered that…

6. Increasing your *cognitive* skills will usually…

7. Hans and Karl liked to indulge in *sophomoric* jokes like…

8. The *nominal* reason the band organized the show was to support a local charity, but…

9. Many people believe that the name "Abraham Lincoln" is *synonymous* with…

10. Barbara became *cognizant* of the other person in the house when…

11. Many donors to charity prefer to remain *anonymous* because…

12. Although the *sophistry* of Alan's argument was clear to some of the audience, others…

Exercise II. Fill in the blank with the best word from the choices below. One word will not be used.

sophisticate   incognito   cognitive   sophomoric   nomenclature

1. The discovery of a new plant species may alter the _____ of the whole category.

2. The advertisement promised that everyone, from simple country folk to stylish _____, would love the circus.

3. In the cartoon, we watched the wolf going _____ in sheep's clothing.

4. The tests the doctor performed showed that Travis's _____ skills were above average for his age, so it was no surprise when he started reading early.

Fill in the blank with the best word from the choices below. One word will not be used.

| cognizant | sophomoric | nominal | denomination | synonymous |

5.   Some people think that marriage is _____ with happiness.

6.   When she became _____ that she was not talented in gymnastics, Lana developed a flair for music.

7.   Beth broke up with her boyfriend for playing a _____ prank on her.

8.   Two _____ of the church gathered to discuss their differences.

Fill in the blank with the best word from the choices below. One word will not be used.

| sophistry | antonym | nominal | incognito | anonymous |

9.   Even people experienced in debate were hypnotized by the _____ of the master speaker.

10.   Although the threatening letter was _____, police eventually traced it to a man who had just been fired from his job.

11.   Mike really wanted to visit Dana, but he had to think up a(n) _____ reason to drop by her house.

12.   We could think of many words similar to the word in question, but not a single _____.

Exercise III. Choose the set of words that best completes the sentence.

1.   Your _____ may fool some of the people some of the time, but most people are _____ of its misleading quality.
     A.   denomination; sophomoric
     B.   sophistry; cognizant
     C.   sophistry; incognito
     D.   nomenclature; cognitive

2.   Jimmy was involved in so many fraternity pranks that his name became _____ with _____ behavior.
     A.   nominal; anonymous
     B.   synonymous; sophomoric
     C.   cognizant; anonymous
     D.   nominal; incognito

3.   For the undercover investigation into illegal businesses, the normally sloppy police officer went _____ as a wealthy _____.
     A.   anonymous; sophistry
     B.   cognizant; sophisticate
     C.   incognito; sophistry
     D.   incognito; sophisticate

4.   Ty's _____ reason for visiting the library was to sharpen his _____ skills, but he was really going to see if Fred had been there.
   A. nominal; cognitive
   B. synonymous; antonym
   C. anonymous; cognitive
   D. sophomoric; anonymous

5.   The _____ used in genetic science was originally developed by a(n) _____ scientist, whose identity is still unknown.
   A. sophisticate; nominal
   B. denomination; synonymous
   C. nomenclature; anonymous
   D. sophistry; cognitive

Exercise IV. Complete the sentence by inferring information about the italicized word from its context.

1.   If Doug criticizes Wally's *sophomoric* behavior at the talent show, Wally may have done things like…

2.   When Jane became *cognizant* that a stranger was following her, she probably…

3.   If Ron says that Pete's *nominal* reason for going to law school was to help people accused of crimes, Ron may be implying that…

Exercise V. Fill in each blank with the word from the Unit that best completes the sentence, using the root we supply as a clue. Then, answer the questions that follow the paragraphs.

Experts in the field of child psychology tell us that before beginning school, the average American child has already spent more hours in television viewing than he or she will spend on formal education. With such _____ (COGN) habits developed at an early age, it is no wonder that many students experience difficulties in school and prove resistant to more formal intellectual stimulation. This early exposure is further enhanced by years of continued television viewing during the formative years of childhood, by movie going and by immersion in contemporary music as the child grows into adolescence and adulthood.

American popular entertainment has even reached beyond the shores of America, becoming an overwhelming force in the cultural life of other nations. The availability of American television programs, movies, and music is more and more an international phenomenon, and it has increasingly displaced local cultural forms. In some countries, this has bred resentment toward the United States, as people see their local cultures changed due to the popularity of American TV, movies, and music.

What upsets many about this triumph of popular entertainment is that much of it is aimed at the lowest common denominator and contains a coarseness and crudity that affects society in negative ways. For increasing numbers of social critics, popular entertainment has become _____ (ONYM) with cultural decay. They see evidence of this decline in social civility, standards of dress, and public and private behavior. While not every negative contemporary phenomenon can be blamed on Hollywood or reality TV, it can certainly be said that popular entertainment has a profound impact on the culture that both produces and consumes it.

1.   According to the passage, American popular entertainment
   A. has been a force for good throughout the world.
   B. has had a profound influence on American and world societies.
   C. has enabled the United States to dominate the world.
   D. has helped children understand the way society works.

2. The author states that some people in other countries resent American popular entertainment because
    A. the United States is the only superpower.
    B. they dislike its content.
    C. it harms their children.
    D. it changes their local cultural institutions.

3. According to the third paragraph, critics of popular entertainment
    A. think it has a negative effect on society.
    B. blame all of society's problems on its influence.
    C. don't like the fact that it is so popular.
    D. think it should be more broadly based.

Exercise VI. Drawing on your knowledge of roots and words in context, read the following selection and define the italicized words. If you cannot figure out the meaning of the words on your own, look them up in a dictionary. Note that *epi* means "upon," and *mis* means "wrong."

The passage of time has demonstrated that the masses value celebrity above all else, as popular entertainment has virtually overwhelmed every other expression of contemporary culture. Super-powerful celebrities have so much name recognition that they can sell albums and movies just by giving them *eponymous* titles. When a rock star calls himself or herself a "god" today, is it really a *misnomer*?

UNIT NINETEEN

MATR
Latin MATER, "mother"

MATRON (mā´ trən) *n.* a married woman
A *matron* in colonial America would have been constantly busy with home and children.

MATERNAL (mə tûr´ nəl) *adj.* having the qualities of a mother; motherly
Even as a child, Bess was *maternal* toward the other students in her class.
syn: nurturing　　　　　　　　*ant: uncaring*

MATRICULATE (mə trik´ yōō lāt) *v.* to enroll in a degree program, especially at a college
Darnell is going to take a year off before he *matriculates* at the business school.

PATR
Latin PATER, "father"

PATRONIZE (pā´ trə nīz) *v.*   1. to regularly visit or give business to
　　　　　　　　　　　　　　　　2. to talk down to; to condescend
1. The Sidlowskis no longer *patronized* the deli.
2. The college professor tried not to *patronize* the high school students.

PATERNAL (pə tûr´ nəl) *adj.* having the qualities of a father
Toby began to feel *paternal* toward the orphaned young boy.

PATRICIDE (pat´ ri sīd) *n.* the murder of a father
L. *pater + cidus,* "murder" = *the murder of a father*
The prince was so jealous of his father that he contemplated *patricide* in order to take over the throne.

EXPATRIATE (eks pā´ trē ət) *n.* a person living outside his or her native country
L. *ex,* "out of" + *patria, (from pater)* "fatherland" = *out of the fatherland*
Gertrude was an *expatriate* who had abandoned America for France.
syn: emigrant　　　　　　　　*ant: native*

After the war, the EX-PATRIOT became an EXPATRIATE and never returned to his native land.

Although the word matriculate is sometimes used to mean "to graduate," it actually means "to join a class or program."

Our human compassion binds us the one to the other—not in pity or patronizingly, but as human beings who have learned how to turn our common suffering into hope for the future.
—Nelson Mandela

A patriarch is the father of a line; for instance, Abraham is said to be the patriarch of the Jews.

FIL
Latin FILIUS, "son; child"

FILIAL   (fil´ ē əl)   *adj.*   having to do with a son or daughter
Carl admitted that he felt more *filial* affection for his stepfather than he did for his father.

AFFILIATE   (ə fil´ ē it)   *n.*   one related to or associated with
L. *ad*, "toward" + *filius* = *like a child toward*
The small business became an *affiliate* of a much larger corporation in New York.
syn: partner   *ant: rival*

GEN
Latin GIGNERE, GENITUS, "give birth to; to create"

PROGENITOR   (prō jen´ ə tər)   *n.*   the founder of a line or race
L. *pro*, "forth" + *gignere* = *one who brings offspring forth*
The *progenitor* of the Louis family in America was a fur merchant named Jacques.
syn: forefather   *ant: descendant*

PROGENY   (präj´ ə nē)   *n.*   children or descendants
At family reunions, the couple always posed for a photograph with their numerous *progeny*.
syn: offspring

GENEALOGY   (jē nē ol´ ə jē)   *n.*   the study of families and descendants
After discovering an old picture of his great uncle, Phillip became interested in the *genealogy* of his family.

▆ *How is progenitor different from* patriarch *on the previous page? You could say that nylon, one of the first completely synthetic fibers for clothing ever produced, was the* progenitor *for acrylics, spandex, Kevlar, and polyesters, but you couldn't say it was the* patriarch.

EXERCISES - UNIT NINETEEN

Exercise I. Complete the sentence in a way that shows you understand the meaning of the italicized vocabulary word.

1.   The *matron* at the jail was assigned…

2.   If the client gets the impression that you are *patronizing* him, he will…

3.   Nathan showed *filial* respect by doing things like…

4.   Some people believe that the Mortenson *progeny* were numerous because…

5.   Harrison plans to *matriculate* at the end of this year so he can…

6.   Walt wonders if his *progenitors* were traveling people because…

7.   Female robins have such a strong *maternal* instinct that…

8.   Because it was an *affiliate* of the national charity, our group…

9.   The older boys in the group always felt *paternal* toward Aaron because…

10.   Thomas was accused of *patricide*, but…

11.   Many famous authors became *expatriates* because…

12.   In researching the historical figure's complex *genealogy*, Jake…

Exercise II. Fill in the blank with the best word from the choices below. One word will not be used.

genealogy   affiliate   maternal   matriculate   matron

1.   However the _____ dressed, she always looked younger than her years.

2.   I wish my _____ was full of interesting characters, but most of my ancestors were simple farmers.

3.   Greta never stopped feeling _____ toward her children, even when they were all grown up.

4.   Right after high school, James tried to _____ into a program for weak readers.

Fill in the blank with the best word from the choices below. One word will not be used.

patronize   progeny   expatriate   affiliate   paternal

5.   Michael was shocked when his longtime _____ was arrested for being a career bank robber.

6.   No one enjoys having a friend who is always _____, even if such condescension is not intentional.

7.   The stable was full of the _____ of the blue-ribbon winner, and several generations lived together.

8.   Sometimes, Arthur and his family considered becoming _____ because they hated the political system in their own country.

Fill in the blank with the best word from the choices below. One word will not be used.

affiliate   patricide   filial   progenitor   paternal

9.   Adult male bears feel little _____ instinct, and they will even attack their own offspring.

10.   The _____ bond between Morgan and her parents was made clear when she thanked them during her valedictorian speech at graduation.

11.   Although Sue sometimes hated her father, she would never consider _____.

12.   A(n) _____ of Benjamin Franklin must have had an inventive spirit, since Franklin himself was so creative.

Exercise III. Choose the set of words that best completes the sentence.

1.   All of the _____ love and gratitude Claude supposedly felt toward his father was proved false when he attempted _____.
     A.   filial; patricide
     B.   paternal; genealogy
     C.   filial; matriculation
     D.   maternal; patricide

2.   Renee was informed that if she legally became a(n) _____, she could no longer be a(n) _____ of the company she worked for in the United States.
     A.   affiliate; patricide
     B.   affiliate; progenitor
     C.   expatriate; affiliate
     D.   expatriate; matron

3.   Do not think that just because you _____ at an expensive and challenging university, you can _____
      those of us who never went to college at all.
      A. matriculated; patronize
      B. patronized; matriculate
      C. affiliated; patronize
      D. patronized; matriculate

4.   Although Mrs. Anderson feels _____ toward all her _____, she has a special feeling for her son Tyrese.
      A. paternal; matrons
      B. maternal; matrons
      C. maternal; progeny
      D. filial; progenitors

5.   When we began examining our family's _____, we discovered that our _____ actually came to the United
      States on the Mayflower.
      A. affiliate; genealogy
      B. matron; expatriate
      C. expatriate; affiliate
      D. genealogy; progenitor

Exercise IV. Complete the sentence by inferring information about the italicized word from its context.

1.   If you are trying to trace your *progenitors* in this country, you will probably need information like…

2.   If someone comments on the remarkably strong *filial* bond between Grace and Danielle, we can assume
      they are…

3.   If the former political prisoner chooses to become an *expatriate* of his country, we can assume he does
      NOT feel…

**Exercise V. Fill in each blank with the word from the Unit that best completes the sentence, using the root
      we supply as a clue. Then, answer the questions that follow the paragraphs.**

The ancient Greek legend of Oedipus serves as a classic example of the use of tragic heroes in literature.

In the legend, Greek oracles, or prophets, foretell that King Laius and Queen Jocasta of Thebes will have a son who will murder his father and marry his mother after growing to manhood. Fearing this prophecy, the king and queen take their infant son to a mountain outside Thebes, nail his feet together, and leave him to die.

A shepherd rescues Oedipus and gives him his name, which means "swollen feet" in Greek. The shepherd brings him to the city of Corinth to be raised as an orphan. King Polybus of Corinth, unable to have his own children, later adopts Oedipus, who is raised as a prince, not knowing who his real parents are.

It isn't until Oedipus becomes a teenager that he learns that he is destined to commit _____ (PATR) by killing his father. Out of _____ (FIL) love for Polybus, Oedipus flees Corinth to prevent the prophecy from coming true. While wandering through Greece, he is attacked by a group of men. King Laius, his real father, is among those he kills in the melee.

Later, Oedipus' wanderings bring him near Thebes, where he meets the Sphinx, a winged monster who is terrorizing the city, devouring all those who can't answer her riddle. Oedipus correctly answers the puzzling question and vanquishes the monster. In gratitude, the people of Thebes name Oedipus king to replace the slain Laius. He later takes Jocasta as his wife, fulfilling the dreaded forecast.

Oedipus rules Thebes wisely for years until a plague hits the city. The oracles warn that the only way to remove the pestilence is to find out who killed King Laius. Oedipus sends his brother-in-law, Creon, to investigate Laius' killing.

Creon returns with the crushing news about Oedipus' true identity and his status as his father's killer.

After learning of their true relationship, a horrified Oedipus blinds himself, while Jocasta hangs herself in shame. Oedipus is exiled and again wanders Greece as a(n) _____ (PATR). After twenty years, he finds sanctuary in the city of Colonus. During Oedipus' exile, the oracles predict that whatever city bears the former king's grave will have eternal prosperity. Creon, who has suc-ceeded Oedipus as Thebes' leader, tries in vain to convince Oedipus to return to his native city. Oedipus, however, dies in Colonus.

Throughout the ages, writers have pointed to Oedipus as a classic example of a tragic figure. Oedipus desired to do good works, but wound up destroying the lives of his father and mother through a combination of circumstance and bad luck. The legend brings to life human fears that powerful forces outside our control can determine our destinies.

1. Which statement best sums up the main idea of the legend of Oedipus?
    A. The oracles' predictions come true in the end.
    B. Prophets always know what the future holds for mankind.
    C. *Bad luck and circumstance can lead good people into tragic situations.*
    D. People bear responsibility for their actions.

2. Oedipus protects King Polybus by
    A. *leaving Corinth and wandering through Greece.*
    B. battling the Sphinx to save Thebes.
    C. blinding himself after learning the truth.
    D. sending Creon to investigate Laius' killing.

3. The Sphinx punishes people for failing her test by
    A. bringing disease into their lives.
    B. denying them access to the city.
    C. turning them to stone.
    D. *devouring them.*

4. Creon wants Oedipus to come home after twenty years of exile because he (Creon)
    A. misses Oedipus.
    B. *is seeking economic gain for Thebes.*
    C. wants Oedipus to retake his throne.
    D. learned about Oedipus' true identity.

Exercise VI. Drawing on your knowledge of roots and words in context, read the following selection and define the italicized words. If you cannot figure out the meaning of the words on your own, look them up in a dictionary. Note that *alma* means "nourishing, supporting," and *arch* means "ruler, leader."

In the year 2000, thirty years after graduation, the members of the class of 1970 returned to their *alma mater* for a reunion. For many, it was the first time back at the college since graduation. As the group shared stories and caught up on each others' lives, they remembered how going to an all-female institution had played a major part in the way they pursued careers in a seemingly *patriarchal* society. Many of the women felt that there was far too much male domination in the world and that something positive needed to be done about it.

UNIT TWENTY

MAGN

Latin MAGNUS, "large; great"

MAGNITUDE   (mag´ ni tōōd)   *n.*   greatness of size, strength, or importance
After the city was rocked by a major earthquake, scientists began to determine the *magnitude* of both the quake and the destruction.
syn: significance   *ant: unimportance*

MAGNATE   (mag´ nāt)   *n.*   an important, powerful person in business
The nineteenth-century railroad *magnates* met to decide the future of American transportation.
syn: baron   *ant: employee*

MAXIM

Latin MAXIMUS, "largest; greatest"

MAXIM   (mak´ sim)   *n.*   a brief statement that conveys a general truth
The *maxim* "Everything in moderation" is especially relevant to undergraduate students.

MIN

Latin MINOR, "less"
Latin MINUERE, MINUTUM, "to lessen"

DIMINISH   (di min´ ish)   *v.*   to make smaller; to lessen
L. *de,* "down" + *minus = down from the smaller*
The area's natural resources will *diminish* quickly unless something is done to preserve them.
syn: reduce   *ant: add, build*

MINUSCULE   (min´ ə skyōōl)   *adj.*   tiny
New electronic devices use only *minuscule* amounts of power, as compared to their predecessors, which needed much more.
syn: insignificant

MINUTE   (mī nōōt´)   *adj.*   extremely small; insignificant
Minute particles of dust or pollen in the air can be enough to trigger a serious allergy attack.
syn: tiny   *ant: enormous*

▣ *The Latin words for* large, larger, *and* largest *are* magnus, major, *and* maximus.

▣ Maxim *comes from a medieval phrase meaning "greatest assertion"; it is a fundamental truth that must be accepted at the beginning of an argument.*

▣ *The Latin words for* small, smaller, *and* smallest *are* parvus, minor, *and* minimus.

MY NEWT is MINUTE, even for a salamander.

MICRO
Greek MICROS, "small"

MICROSCOPIC (mī krə skäp´ ik) *adj.*   done with attention to small details
G. *micros* + *skopein*, "to look" = *to look at very small things*
After five years of *microscopic* analysis of the problem, the researchers still had no certain answers.
syn: painstaking   *ant: careless*

MICROCOSM (mī´ krə kozm) *n.*   a small model of a larger pattern or place
G. *micros* + *cosmos*, "world" = *small world*
Some people believe that an individual's actions are merely a *microcosm* of the actions of society.

MEGA
Greek MEGALOS, "large"

MEGALOPOLIS (meg ə läp´ ə ləs) *n.*   a very large city
G. *megalos* + *polis*, "city" = *large city*
Lost in the *megalopolis*, the tourists searched frantically for a cab or a phone.

MEGALOMANIAC (meg ə lō mā´ nē ak) *n.*   one who believes him or herself
        all-powerful or indestructible
Most historians believe that Adolf Hitler is the perfect example of a *megalomaniac.*

▥ *A microbe (from micro + bios, "life") is an organism too small to be seen without magnification.*

▥ *Even though it is not a single city, the area from Boston to Washington, DC, including New York City, Philadelphia, and Baltimore, is considered a megalopolis. More than 17% of the US population lives in this area.*

EXERCISES - UNIT TWENTY

Exercise I. Complete the sentence in a way that shows you understand the meaning of the italicized vocabulary word.

1.   The *magnitude* of the economic crisis became clear when…

2.   His friends called him a *megalomaniac* every time he…

3.   The wealthiest leaders at the economic conference this year are oil *magnates* because…

4.   New York City can accurately be called a *megalopolis* because…

5.   The politician began his speech by quoting a *maxim* that stated…

6.   Although the stranded hikers' food supply had *diminished*,…

7.   Because local governments can be viewed as a *microcosm* of the national government,…

8.   The particles of the meteor discovered embedded in the earth were so *minute* that…

9.   Only a careful, *microscopic* analysis will provide answers to the problem of…

10. Because his contribution to the company's success was so *minuscule*, Quentin…

Exercise II. Fill in the blank with the best word from the choices below. One word will not be used.

microcosm   maxim   magnate   megalomaniac

1.   Herbert was becoming more like a _____ by the day, and his employees began to grow afraid of him.

2.   Terry was fast becoming a shoe _____; he owned almost a hundred shoe stores around the country.

3.   Searching for a _____ that would appeal to his own life, James discovered that "It is better to ask forgiveness than permission."

Fill in the blank with the best word from the choices below. One word will not be used.

magnitude   diminish   minute   megalopolis   microcosm

4.   The small aquarium was a _____ of life in the great oceans.

5.   Although I did not win first place, nothing could _____ the pride I felt in performing well.

6.   Since no one knew how much had been stolen, the _____ of the crime was unknown.

7.   Even very _____ amounts of the chemical dust can cause serious harm.

Fill in the blank with the best word from the choices below. One word will not be used.

megalopolis   microscopic   minuscule   diminish

8.   The judge assured us that the difference between "Very Good" and "Excellent" was _____.

9.   Living in a _____ has some advantages, but you may tire of the crowds.

10. A _____ examination revealed some subtle flaws in the witness's story.

Exercise III. Choose the set of words that best completes the sentence.

1.   The lobbyist warns that if we can't find a way to _____ the power of the oil _____, we will never see lower gasoline prices.
     A.   diminish; microcosm
     B.   diminish; megalopolis
     C.   diminish; magnates
     D.   diminish; magnitudes

2.   Stan is such a _____ that everyone else's problems seem _____ to him.
     A.   microcosm; microscopic
     B.   megalopolis; minuscule
     C.   magnate; diminished
     D.   megalomaniac; minuscule

3.   Students who adhere to the _____ "The devil is in the details" will avoid getting bogged down in _____ particulars.
     A.   magnate; minuscule
     B.   maxim; minute
     C.   microcosm; minute
     D.   maxim; minuscule

4. Is a small town a _____ of a huge, busy _____, or do they not fit the same pattern?
    A. magnate; microcosm
    B. microcosm; megalopolis
    C. megalomaniac; microcosm
    D. microcosm; magnate

5. The greater the _____ of a war, the more the planners of the war must go into _____ detail in their strategy.
    A. magnitude; microscopic
    B. microcosm; minuscule
    C. megalopolis; microscopic
    D. megalomaniac; minute

Exercise IV. Complete the sentence by inferring information about the italicized word from its context.

1. If a group makes an effort to *diminish* the reputation of the mayor, he might…

2. If money is of *minuscule* importance to Sam, he may choose a job that…

3. If Eleanor says that George ignores every *maxim* she quotes, we can assume that George thinks…

Exercise V. Fill in each blank with the word from the Unit that best completes the sentence, using the root we supply as a clue. Then, answer the questions that follow the paragraphs.

Over ten million Americans have Age-related Macular Degeneration, or AMD, a disease that causes a slow, progressive loss of vision. The sight of an individual with macular degeneration _____ (MIN) over time. The person does not have a total loss of sight, but experiences distorted or blurred vision. The symptoms he or she experiences are the opposite of "tunnel vision" in which the person cannot see peripherally, only in a central area of the field of vision; with AMD, the sufferer loses the center. This results in an inability to drive, read, or even recognize faces. Most people with macular degeneration are aged 50 and older; it is the leading cause of blindness for people aged 70 and older, affecting nearly 12% of that population.

The exact causes of AMD are unknown, and it has no cure at present. There are a number of risk factors that are believed to be associated with macular degeneration, however. Some researchers think that the disease is caused by genetic factors. Current studies are also examining whether certain environmental factors such as smoking and diet have an effect on human sight. If so, it may be possible to prevent or slow the damaging effects of AMD by following certain nutritional guidelines. Researchers also theorize that sun exposure may cause damage to the eye and lead to the disease. If an individual who may be at risk for developing macular degeneration is aware that some of these environmental factors can be controlled, he or she may be able to prevent the development of the disease.

Once a person has developed macular degeneration, though, eyesight cannot be totally repaired, but there are a number of treatments available. Laser surgery can be used to treat some forms of the disease. There are also a number of aids that can help a person see better. Because the ability to see to the side still exists, glasses and special lenses can enhance the person's limited vision. There are also adaptions for computers, reading machines, and print enlargers available to read small print. Another option is to mount a tiny magnifier on a pair of glasses that will enable a person to see objects more clearly, even something _____ (MIN). Unfortunately, though aids may help to correct the vision of a person suffering from AMD, it doesn't correct eyesight completely. With current treatments, the person suffering from macular degeneration must learn to deal with the vision loss as best as possible.

1.   Based on information in the passage, with which statement would the author agree?
     A. Environmental factors play an important role in AMD.
     B. AMD is now affecting more and more people.
     C. Tunnel vision reduces eyesight similarly to AMD.
     D. A small telescope attached to glasses can help AMD.

2.   According to the passage, what factor is believed to cause age-related macular degeneration?
     A. dust particles
     B. childhood illness
     C. reading under bad light
     D. exposure to the sun

3.   Which one of the following is NOT a way that vision aids can help the eyesight of a person suffering
     from macular degeneration?
     A. They enlarge small print.
     B. They allow blurred objects to be seen more clearly.
     C. They prevent declining vision.
     D. They enhance existing vision.

4.   Which statement below is true?
     A. A cure for AMD may soon be available.
     B. Diet plays a big role in developing AMD.
     C. AMD does not cause a loss of peripheral vision.
     D. Twelve percent of people currently have AMD.

**Exercise VI. Drawing on your knowledge of roots and words in context, read the following selection and
     define the italicized words. If you cannot figure out the meaning of the words on your own, look them
     up in a dictionary. Note that *opus* means "work," and *animus* means "soul."**

     The film *Mr. Holland's Opus* deals with a high school music teacher's quest to raise a family, make a difference
in the lives of his students, and write a symphony. During the final scene of the movie, Mr. Holland's *magnum
opus* is brought to life by his many former and current students. His work, "An American Symphony," proves
that a man with a dream can accomplish a feat of great importance. Audiences continue to remain in awe of the
magnanimous spirit in the seemingly ordinary body of Mr. Holland long after the last note of the music.

VOCABULARY WORD LIST FOR BOOKS IN THIS SERIES

Level VII

abbreviate
abduct
absolute
accessible
accompaniment
adjacent
aerate
aerial
affection
affirmative
agenda
airy
alleviate
ambition
analogy
apologetic
appendix
application
apprehend
ascertain
asocial
aspire
associate
assumption
attentive
attractive
ballistic
biographical
brevity
brutality
brute
capacity
capitalize
captivate
celebrant
celebratory
celebrity
certainty
certify
circumstance
coagulate
companionship
complex
composition
comprehend
compute
concerted
condense
conduct
confidante
confident
confirm
conscience
conservative
constant
constrict
consume
contract
convection
convict
cooperate
course
creed
currency
decapitate
deficient
deflate
defunct

deliverance
delude
denounce
density
deposit
descriptive
diagram
discount
discredit
disintegrate
dismantle
dispense
distract
domestic
domicile
dominate
dominion
duplicate
effortless
elevate
elongate
emaciated
emancipate
encompass
evaluate
evict
exhilarating
expire
fabled
fabulous
facsimile
fortify
fortitude
frugal
fruitful
gradual
grave
gravity
hilarity
host
hostile
hyperventilate
ideal
idealistic
idealize
illogical
illusion
impermanent
impress
incredible
infirm
inflate
inoperable
integrate
integrity
intend
invalid
invaluable
jubilant
jubilee
leverage
levitate
liberal
liberate
linguistic
literal
literate
malfunction
mantled

manual
manufacture
manuscript
meager
militant
militarize
multilingual
mythical
mythology
narrate
narrative
obliterate
observant
occurrence
omnipotent
operational
opponent
oppress
oral
oration
oratory
parable
passable
petrify
possessive
potent
preservation
presumptuous
procession
produce
program
progression
projectile
prolong
pronounce
proposition
prosecute
rapidity
rapture
recipient
recount
recurrent
regal
regicide
reign
remnant
reputation
restriction
reveal
savor
savvy
scientific
sensation
sensible
sentimental
sequel
sequence
sociable
socialize
solution
spirited
stationary
status
subject
subscribe
succession
suffice
sumptuous
suspend

symbolize
textile
texture
transact
transgress
transit
unveil
validate
vehicle
ventilate
victorious

Level VIII

abhor
abundant
accelerated
administer
admission
advisable
agile
agitate
allege
amnesty
anarchy
annals
annual
annuity
antediluvian
anticipate
appreciative
arbiter
arbitrary
arbitrate
archaic
arid
aspersion
assiduous
astronomical
autonomous
avail
castigate
cataclysmic
celestial
censor
censure
chastened
chastise
chronic
chronology
cloister
cohabitation
commensurate
composure
conceive
condone
confines
connoisseur
consolidate
conspicuous
contemporaneous
contemporary
corroborate
deceptive
deify
deign
deity
deluge
demented
demote

depreciate
derivative
desist
despicable
deter
detract
diagnosis
differentiate
dilute
dimension
disclose
discourse
disdain
disperse
dissident
donor
durable
duration
editorial
emergent
enact
enduring
energetic
enumerate
ergonomic
evident
exaggerated
exceptional
excursion
exhibit
exhume
exponential
extol
extract
finite
formidable
forte
fortitude
founder
frequent
fugitive
fundamental
fusion
horrific
humility
hypothesis
idiom
idiosyncrasy
immense
immerse
immovable
imposition
impunity
inconstant
indeterminate
indignant
infrequent
ingest
innumerable
inoculate
insidious
instantaneous
insular
insulate
inter
intercept
interminable
intersperse
intimidate

intrepid
intuitive
inveterate
invigorate
irreverent
jurisdiction
jurisprudence
litigant
litigation
magisterial
magistrate
matriarch
mentality
minister
mnemonic
mobile
monotheism
nebulous
nemesis
nimbus
nonplussed
nontraditional
notorious
ocular
omission
pantheon
parenthetical
participant
perjure
persistent
plurality
polytheistic
preliminary
preside
prodigal
prognosis
punitive
ration
rational
reactionary
reconnaissance
redundant
reference
refine
refuge
refuse
reinstate
repository
residual
respective
revere
revise
rivulet
robust
sanctify
sanctions
sanctuary
sanctum
seclude
sedentary
single
singular
solidarity
sparse
stellar
subliminal
submerge
submissive
subpoena

subsidiary
subsist
subterfuge
subterranean
suggestible
supersede
surgical
surplus
suspect
syndicate
synthesize
tempo
terminal
terrestrial
terrorize
timorous
torrent
torrid
trepidation
tutelage
unrivaled
valiant
valor
veteran
vigorous
vista
volatile

Level IX

abjure
abstain
accord
adept
affable
affiliate
affluent
agenda
alias
alienate
allegation
alleviate
alteration
altercation
alternate
amble
ambulatory
amiable
amicable
analogous
animosity
anonymous
antagonist
antagonize
antebellum
antibiotic
antonym
aptitude
aristocracy
assonance
audit
auditory
bellicose
belligerence
benefactor
benevolent
benign
bibliophile
biodegradable
bureaucrat

cadence
casualty
cede
circumspect
cognitive
cognizant
collapse
concession
confound
conjure
consecutive
cordial
corporeal
corpulent
courier
decadent
delegate
denomination
deplete
dialogue
dictum
digress
dilate
diminish
discord
disenchanted
dismal
dispel
disposition
dissemble
dissonance
divest
domineering
edict
effigy
elapse
elucidate
enamored
enjoin
enunciate
equanimity
equilibrium
equitable
exacting
execution
expatriate
expedient
figment
filial
formative
genealogy
gradualism
herbivorous
homogenized
homonym
immortalize
impart
impartial
impediment
implement
impose
improvise
inalienable
inaudible
incantation
incision
inclusive
incognito
inconclusive

inconsequential
incorporate
incur
indecisive
indict
indomitable
ineffable
inept
infantile
infuse
inhibit
iniquity
injunction
invidious
invoke
leaven
legacy
legislative
legitimize
levity
lucid
magnanimous
magnate
magnitude
malevolent
malicious
maternal
matriculate
matron
maxim
megalomaniac
megalopolis
mellifluous
metabolism
metamorphosis
metaphorical
microcosm
microscopic
miniscule
minute
misinformation
monogamy
monolithic
monologue
monopolize
morbid
moribund
mortify
nomenclature
nominal
noxious
omnivorous
partisan
paternal
patricide
patronize
pedagogue
pedant
pedestrian
perceptible
perjury
pernicious
philanthropy
philosophical
phosphorescent
photogenic
phototropic
posit
preamble

precept
precise
preclude
predominant
prefigure
privileged
proactive
progenitor
progeny
prohibit
prologue
pronouncement
propel
prospect
protagonist
providential
provocative
rapacious
rapt
recant
recede
recurrent
reform
regress
rejoinder
relapse
relative
renounce
replete
repulsion
resonant
retinue
revival
revoke
semblance
simulate
sophisticate
sophistry
sophomoric
specter
suffuse
superfluous
superlative
surreptitious
susceptible
sustain
symbiotic
synonymous
tenacious
theocracy
translucent
travesty
unanimous
uniform
unison
vested
vestment
vivacious
vivid
voracious

Level X
aberrant
abject
abrogate
acerbic
acquisitive
acrid
acrimonious

adherent
admonition
adverse
advocate
aesthetic
anatomy
anesthetic
annotate
antipathy
apathetic
apolitical
apparition
approbation
arrogant
aspect
avarice
avid
benediction
bibulous
cautionary
cautious
circumvent
civic
civility
civilize
clamorous
colloquial
compel
complacent
comportment
compunction
conciliatory
concise
conducive
confer
confide
congress
conjecture
connotation
conscientious
constructive
construe
convene
convoluted
correspond
cosmopolitan
counsel
covenant
credence
credible
credulity
crucial
crux
culpable
culprit
cursory
declaim
decriminalize
deduce
defer
deference
definitive
deflect
degrade
dejected
demagogue
demographic
denotation
deprecate

derogatory
despondent
destitute
deviate
diaphanous
dichotomy
dictate
diffident
diffuse
diligent
dismissive
dispute
disreputable
dissolute
dissuade
docile
doctrine
doleful
dolorous
dubious
effervescent
effusive
egress
eloquent
emissary
emote
empathy
envisage
epiphany
epitome
equivocate
errant
erroneous
espouse
evince
evocative
evolve
exacerbate
excise
exclamatory
excruciating
exonerate
expel
expound
extort
facile
facsimile
factotum
fallacious
fallacy
fallible
fervent
fervor
fetid
fidelity
fractious
glut
glutton
gratuitous
gustatory
gusto
imbibe
impervious
impetuous
impetus
imprecation
impulse
impute
incisive

incoherent
incredulous
incriminate
incursion
indoctrinate
indolent
indubitable
induce
inference
infinite
infinitesimal
inflection
inflexible
infraction
infrastructure
infringe
ingrate
ingratiate
inherent
innovative
inquisitive
insipid
insoluble
intact
intemperate
interrogate
intractable
introspective
invincible
irrational
locution
malediction
malodorous
mea culpa
motif
motive
novel
novice
obviate
odoriferous
olfactory
onerous
onus
palatable
palate
pandemic
pathos
penultimate
perspicacious
persuasion
petulant
phenomenon
placebo
placid
politicize
precarious
precaution
precursor
premonition
prescient
presentiment
primacy
primal
primeval
proffer
proficient
profuse
proliferate
proponent

protracted
provincial
punctilious
pungent
purported
putrefy
putrid
rancid
rancor
rationale
rationalize
recollect
reconcile
recourse
recrimination
redolent
redoubtable
remiss
reprobate
reprove
requisition
resolute
restitution
retort
retract
retrospective
revert
sacrilege
sapient
sentient
sentiment
sentinel
stagnant
stagnate
stature
subvert
sycophant
tactile
tangible
temper
temperance
tome
tortuous
ultimate
ultimatum
unconscionable
viaduct
virile
virtue
virtuoso
visage
voluble

Level XI
ablution
abominable
abomination
accede
acclivity
acquiesce
adorn
adventitious
alluvial
ambiance
annex
antecedent
appall
append
appraise

appreciable
apropos
ascertain
assertion
attrition
auspices
auspicious
bacchanal
bacchic
belabor
candid
candor
catholic
cavernous
certitude
circuitous
communal
concave
conferment
conflagration
congested
consort
consortium
consummate
contort
contravene
contrite
converge
crevasse
crevice
declivity
decorous
decorum
demerit
demonstrative
denigrate
depose
deracinate
desolate
destine
desultory
detrimental
detritus
discomfit
disconcert
disseminate
dissertation
distill
distort
diverge
divulge
ecstasy
edification
elaborate
elegiac
elegy
entity
eradicate
essence
euphoria
excavate
excommunicate
exertion
expendable
extant
exultant
feasible
festoon
fete

fission
fissure
flagrant
flamboyant
florid
flourish
fluctuate
fluent
formality
formulaic
formulate
fortuitous
fortuity
fulminate
germane
germinal
germinate
gestate
gesticulate
hiatus
hoi polloi
holistic
illustrative
illustrious
impair
impeccable
impending
implicit
importunate
importune
incandescent
incendiary
incense
incommunicado
inexplicable
inflammatory
inordinate
insinuate
instill
insufferable
interject
inundate
irradicable
jocose
jocular
laborious
lachrymal
lachrymose
languid
languish
languor
lavish
lenient
lenitive
lethargy
liaison
ligature
liturgy
livid
luster
magnum opus
malaise
malfeasance
malign
malinger
meander
meretricious
meritorious
metaphrase

modus operandi
mollify
monosyllabic
monotone
monotonous
munificent
negate
negligent
negligible
nexus
obligatory
ominous
opulent
ordain
orifice
ornate
orotund
pallid
pallor
paradigm
paraphrase
parcel
parse
parvenu
peccadillo
peccant
pejorative
periphery
phraseology
plaint
plaintive
polyglot
polymath
precedent
predestine
preferential
preordained
proclivity
propitiate
propitious
quintessential
quittance
rapport
redound
refulgent
remonstrate
remunerate
repartee
requiem
resilient
restive
riparian
rudiment
rudimentary
sedition
semantic
seminal
semiotic
sinuous
soliloquy
solipsism
somnolent
sopor
soporific
stanch
stasis
static
staunch
subjective

suborn
summation
surfeit
synergy
totalitarian
totality
transitory
trenchant
trite
truncate
undulate
verdant
verdure
vigilant
vigilante
viridity
vulgar

Level XII
abscond
abstruse
adduce
adjourn
adjudicate
adroit
adumbrate
aggregate
agrarian
alacrity
allocate
allude
amoral
anachronism
anathema
animadversion
aperture
apocryphal
apposite
apprise
artifice
artless
ascribe
aspire
assay
asset
attenuate
avocation
bucolic
capitulate
caprice
celerity
chronicle
circumlocution
circumscribe
cogent
cognate
colloquy
collusion
complicity
composite
comprise
concede
concordance
concur
confluence
conjugal
consecrate
consign
conspire

constrain
contend
context
contiguous
contingent
covert
cryptic
defray
degenerate
demise
demur
demure
derisive
devoid
diabolical
discern
discordant
discrete
discretion
discursive
distend
diurnal
dour
duplicitous
duress
dystopian
egregious
emblematic
emulate
engender
ensue
episodic
epithet
esprit
evanescent
execrable
exigent
expiate
explicate
extemporaneous
extenuating
feign
felicitous
felicity
fictive
flux
fruition
fruitless
genre
gregarious
hyperbole
icon
iconoclast
iconography
idyllic
impious
implicate
in lieu of
inanimate
incessant
incite
inconsolable
incorrigible
incurious
inert
inexplicable
infelicitous
influx
infrangible

inimitable
innate
innocuous
insatiable
insuperable
intercede
interlude
internecine
interpose
intransigent
intrusive
inveigh
irrepressible
judicious
locus
loquacious
ludicrous
magniloquent
methodical
moratorium
mores
morose
myopic
nascent
obdurate
obloquy
obsequious
obtrusive
ostensible
overt
parturient
pastoral
peregrination
perpetuate
perpetuity
pertinacious
perturb
plenary
plenipotentiary
portend
precipitate
prestige
pretext
procure
proscribe
proviso
psyche
psychosomatic
psychotic
purveyor
purview
pusillanimous
recapitulate
recondite
rectify
rectitude
refract
remit
repast
repertory
reprehensible
reprimand
reserved
resignation
resuscitate
reticent
risible
rustic
sacrosanct

salubrious
salutary
salutation
satiety
sectarian
segue
servile
signatory
sinecure
sojourn
solace
solicitous
sovereign
stricture
stringent
subdue
subjugate
subservient
subtext
succor
suffrage
suppress
surfeit
surmise
synchronous
synod
synopsis
tacit
taciturn
temporal
temporize
tenable
tendentious
tenet
tenuous
topical
traduce
transect
transfigure
transpire
turbid
turbulent
umbrage
univocal
utopian
vacuity
vacuous
vaunted
vehement
verbatim
verbiage
verbose
vocation
vociferous